LANGUAGE OF THE SELF

FRITHJOF SCHUON

Revised Translation

WORLD WISDOM BOOKS, INC.

Library of Congress Cataloging-in-Publication Data

Schuon, Frithjof, 1907-1998
  [Essays. French. Selections]
  Language of the self / Frithjof Schuon.
    p. cm.
  "Revised translation."
  Translated from French.
  Includes bibliographical references and index.
  ISBN 0-941532-26-7 (alk. paper)
  1. Religion—Philosophy.   2. Philosophy, Indic.   I. Title.
BL51.S4647 1999
200—dc21   98-40021
                                                  CIP

The photograph on the cover is a detail from the
Temple of the Sun at Konarak, India.
By permission of the photographer, Erwin Böhm

Printed on acid-free paper in The United States of America

For information address World Wisdom Books, Inc.
P. O. Box 2682, Bloomington, Indiana 47402-2682
http://www.worldwisdom.com

This book is dedicated to
His Holiness the Jagadguru
Shrī Shankarāchārya Svāmigal
of Kānchī Kāmakoti Pītha
*who has kindly accepted the offering**

*Dedication to the 1959 edition

Contents

Foreword
to the Revised Translation

At the beginning of the twentieth century, a school of thought arose with René Guénon and Ananda Coomaraswamy which has focused on the enunciation and explanation of the *Philosophia Perennis*; this philosophy is the timeless metaphysical truth underlying the diverse religions, and whose written sources are the revealed Scriptures as well as the writings of the great spiritual masters. Because these truths are permanent and universal, the point of view may thus be called "Perennialist." Frithjof Schuon is by far the pre-eminent spokesman and exponent of the "Perennialist Perspective," having written more than twenty books on this subject; these books as a whole can be said to contain the Perennialist Philosophy.

The first edition of *Language of the Self* appeared in 1959, published by Ganesh and Co. in Madras. Since that time, the importance of this perspective has become all the more clear in a world increasingly dominated by conflicting confessional fanaticisms and by unbelief. It is in the light of the *Philosophia Perennis*, which views every religion "from within," that may be found the keys for an adequate understanding which, joined to the sense of the sacred, alone can safeguard the irreplaceable values and genuine spiritual possibilities of the great religions.

Schuon's outlook is very much that of the *Sanātana Dharma*, and his message has three main dimensions: comprehension, concentration, conformation. Comprehension of the Truth; concentration on the Truth through methodical and quintessential prayer; conformation to these dimensions through intrinsic morality, which means beauty of character. Without this beauty, there can be no serious assimilation of the metaphysical truth, nor any efficacious method of orison. To these may be added a fourth and more extrinsic element: the beauty of our ambiance and hence our affinity with virgin Nature. For as Plato expressed it: "Beauty is the splendor or the True."

Reviews of Schuon's works have recently begun to appear in Indian intellectual journals, with an evident appreciation for the re-establishment of the sapiential core of traditionalism. In view of this interest, the initial translation has been revised, and the editors are pleased to present — simultaneously with the appearance of a new Indian edition — this new edition of *Language of the Self.*

LANGUAGE OF THE SELF

Orthodoxy and Intellectuality

Orthodoxy is the principle of formal homogeneity proper to any authentically spiritual perspective; it is therefore an indispensable aspect of all genuine intellectuality, which is to say that the essence of every orthodoxy is the truth and not mere fidelity to a system that eventually turns out to be false. To be orthodox means to participate, by way of a doctrine that can properly be called "traditional," in the immutability of the principles which govern the Universe and fashion our intelligence.

What perhaps renders somewhat difficult the definition of orthodoxy is that in fact it presents two principal modes, one being essential or intrinsic and the other formal or extrinsic: the latter concerns its accordance with truth in some particular revealed form, the former its accordance with essential and universal truth, whether or not this agrees with a given particular form, so that these two modes may sometimes oppose one another outwardly. For example, Buddhism is on the one hand extrinsically heterodox in relation to Hinduism, because it is separated from the basic forms of the latter, and on the other hand it is intrinsically orthodox because it accords with the universal truth from which it derives. By contrast, the Brahmo-samāj, like every other form of "progressive" neo-Hinduism, is heterodox twice over, firstly in relation to Hinduism and secondly in relation to truth itself, heterodox therefore both from the particular point of view of form and from the universal

1

point of view of essence. A *sannyāsi* may disregard caste
without thereby departing from brahmanical orthodoxy,
since this orthodoxy recognizes all spiritual possibilities;
but if he preaches the abolition of the Hindu social system
he is a heretic, for then he is setting himself up against the
Revelation, the form "willed by God," or rather one of the
forms, for none of them is exclusive. True, the exception
proves the rule, that is to say the limitlessness of All-Possibility requires exceptions, and these therefore will occur
also in the field of orthodoxy, as is shown by Kabir for
example; but here, precisely, the apparent heresy is only on
the level of form, without the intrusion of any intrinsically
false idea or attitude.[1]

Objections will no doubt be made that Hindu spirituality
does not know orthodoxy, since opinions and systems contradict one another in Hinduism even more than in any
other traditional wisdom; rightly or wrongly, according to
the individual, it will be claimed that the "great thinkers"
of India are beyond forms and so are free from all "narrow
dogmatism."[2] It is true that Hindu orthodoxy is sometimes
more difficult to grasp from outside than that of a monotheist tradition; this is because Hinduism is founded more
directly on the metaphysical essence, so that the form can
be treated more freely; also, dogma — or what corresponds
to it — assumes forms more varied than in Western religions, which amounts to saying, not that Hinduism is not

---

1. Kabir incarnates not a form or a theory, but an essence or a realization; he is the exceptional, but necessary, manifestation of the non-formal
link between Hindu *bhakti* and Islamic *mahabbah*; a case such as his could
not fail to occur in a place like India which was Brahmanical and Moslem
at the same time. In other words, Kabir's *bhakti* is exceptional because it
has no formal framework, and it is necessary because dictated by the
spiritual circumstances and, above all, by the limitlessness of the divine
Possibility.

2. Westernized heretics are placed on the same level as the most
venerable authorities of the Vedic tradition; the "breadth of mind"
boasted by the moderns profits nothing except error and unintelligence.

2

quite orthodox, but that its orthodoxy has a wider scope in respect of form, which is all that is in question here.[3]

The wide range of forms belonging to Hinduism may be bewildering to some minds, but could never mean that Hinduism sanctions error, as is in fact done by modern philosophy, where "genius" and "culture" count as much as, or more than, truth and where the very idea of truth is even called into question by some people. The formal "fluidity" proper to Hinduism in no way prevents error from being always recognizable, whether by the aid of scriptural criteria, or in the light of metaphysical truth, which immediately unmasks absurdity, even when heterodoxy is founded on a sacred text, this of course through falsifying its meaning. The doctrines of *jñāna* and *bhakti* contradict one another outwardly because of the difference of levels and modes, but neither is absurd in itself: to say that the world is unreal, or that it is real, or that it is both at once, or again that it is neither one nor the other, is true according to the perspective adopted, and these perspectives result from objective reality and not from human arbitrariness. Intrinsic heterodoxy is, we repeat, contrary not only to a particular perspective or a particular formulation, but to the very nature of things, for it results, not from a perspective legitimate by nature and therefore "providential," but from the arbitrary judgment of a mind left to its own resources and obliged to "create" what the intellect when paralyzed — fundamentally or accidentally — cannot transmit to it. When a man seeks to escape from dogmatic narrowness it is essential that it be "upwards" and not "downwards": dogmatic form is transcended by fathoming

3. Hinduism, despite its extreme conceptual "elasticity," does not swallow everything, for otherwise Jainism and Buddhism would have become additional *darshanas* instead of being excluded from specifically Hindu orthodoxy; on the other hand, the very breadth of this orthodoxy allows it to recognize a posteriori — but "on the margin" and without any innovation — the celestial character both of the Buddha and of his message.

its depths and contemplating its universal content, and not by denying it in the name of a pretentious and iconoclastic ideal of "pure truth."[4]

It is also necessary to take account of the differentiated manifestation of the total doctrine: if "the divergences of theologians are a blessing," as Moslems say, this means that the total doctrine, contained more or less synthetically in the Revelation, is only rendered explicit by "fragments" which are outwardly divergent, although fundamentally concordant. The totality in question does not relate to the intrinsic truth but to the human possibilities of understanding and realization; it is obvious that in respect of quality the perspective of Shankara, for example, is "total," and therefore it contains eminently the perspective of Ramanuja, since it goes beyond it: but its formulation could not take account of all possible levels of truth, so that the perspective of Ramanuja becomes necessary. This leads us to point out that an intellectual authority is infallible within the framework assigned to him by the tradition, and on this plane alone; he can assuredly be infallible beyond this framework and on all planes, but is not necessarily so, firstly because no man can a priori have knowledge of all the elements of truth, and secondly because intellectual intuition may on occasion operate more easily in one given dimension than in some other, according to the nature of the human receptacle.

When we say that a doctrine is providential, we mean by this that it is contained in its own way in the Revelation itself and that it cannot fail to be "crystallized" at the cyclic moment assigned to it by its nature; thus, *bhakti* has always existed as a spiritual possibility, but its flowering required particular conditions, belonging to a given phase of the Hindu cycle. Every cycle has qualitative aspects: what is

4. Within the monotheist religions, sapiential esoterism inevitably presents aspects of extrinsic heterodoxy, for a qualitative difference necessarily shows aspects of opposition.

possible at a certain moment is not possible at another, so that the birth of a particular perspective cannot occur at some arbitrary moment. And this provides us with yet another criterion of orthodoxy — or of heterodoxy — for it is certain that in our times, that is for the last few centuries, the cyclic moment for the manifestation of the great perspectives *(darshanas)* is past; readaptations — in the sense of a legitimate and therefore adequate and efficacious synthesis — are always possible, but not the manifestations of perspectives that are fundamental and "new" as to their form.

The least that can be said is that no present formulation could surpass the ancient formulations; commentaries can be made on the traditional perspectives, they can be summed up from a particular point of view or expressed according to a particular inspiration, but they cannot be contradicted or replaced. It was possible, for example, for Ramanuja to contradict Shankara on the basis of a perspective which, though doubtless limited, was legitimate on its own level and "willed by God"; but no man of our times is a Ramanuja, that is to say there is no one who can reject Shankara except he do so in the footsteps of Ramanuja and within his doctrinal limits, on the level, that is of traditional *bhakti*; he could not surpass both Shankara's *jnāna* and Ramanuja's *bhakti* at the same time, claiming to classify them and to add to them a new and better element. The spuriousness of such attempts always shows itself — apart from intrinsic errors — in the belittling and falsifying spirit which is so characteristic of the modern world; in fact it requires a prodigious lack of spiritual sensibility and of sense of proportion to take any contemporary thinking, even the best possible, for one of the great providential "crystallizations" of the *philosophia perennis*.

*
*   *

This question of the limitations of Ramanuja's outlook — or of *bhakti* in general — obliges us to point out that in order to avoid some quite unjustifiable confusions a distinction must be made between two degrees of doctrinal limitation which are eminently unequal: in the first case, the doctrine accepts certain restrictions in view of particular mental conditions or a particular spiritual method; in the second case, it is intrinsically false; there lies the whole difference between lesser truth and error. The first limitation is to some extent dictated by the needs of a particular mentality, and is thus "willed by God" — whether it is a question of Ramanuja or of Aristotle, to cite two very different cases — whereas the second springs from human weakness and also from the devil, who exploits this weakness, and who cannot but exploit it. In other words, two doctrines may be opposed to one another either because of a legitimate difference of perspective,[5] or because one of them is erroneous, or because both are so but in different ways; care must therefore be taken to avoid putting oppositions of form on the same level with fundamental contradictions.

It is not possible to emphasize too strongly that philosophy, in its humanistic and rationalizing and therefore current sense, consists primarily of logic; this definition of Guénon's correctly situates philosophical thought in making clear its distinction from "intellectual intuition," which is direct perception of truth. But another distinction must also be established on the rational plane itself: logic can

---

5. When Averroes asserts the unity of the intellect and apparently seems to deny the immortality of the individual soul, he is right in the sense that the one, universal Intellects exists — particular intelligences being luminous thanks to it alone — and that the purely sentient part of the soul is in fact perishable; but his opponents also are right in the sense that the diversification of the intelligence and the immortality of the human person are incontestable realities. The specifically philosophical or logical point of view — apart from all question of spiritual opportuneness — is characterized by its incapacity to reconcile antinomic truths, an incapacity deriving from the very nature of reason.

either operate in accordance with an intellection or on the contrary put itself at the disposal of an error, so that philosophy can become the vehicle of just about anything; it may be an Aristotelianism conveying ontological knowledge, just as it may degenerate into an existentialism in which logic is no more than a blind, unreal activity, and which can rightly be described as an "esoterism of stupidity." When unintelligence — and what we mean by this is in no way incompatible with "worldly" intelligence — joins with passion to prostitute logic, it is impossible to escape a mental satanism which destroys the very basis of intelligence and truth.

The validity of a logical demonstration depends then on the prior knowledge which this demonstration aims at communicating, and it is clearly false to take as the point of departure, not a direct cognition, but logic pure and simple; when man has no "visionary" — as opposed to discursive — knowledge of Being, and when he thinks only with his brain instead of "seeing" with the "heart," all his logic will be useless to him, since he starts from an initial blindness. A further distinction must be made between the validity of a demonstration and its dialectical efficacy; the latter evidently depends on an intuitive disposition for recognizing the truth demonstrated, namely on intellectual capacity, which amounts to saying that a demonstration is effective for those to whom it applies. Logic is nothing other than the science of mental coordination, of rational conclusion; hence it cannot attain to the universal and the transcendent by its own resources; a supralogical — but not "illogical" — dialectic based on symbolism and on analogy, and therefore descriptive rather than ratiocinative, may be harder for some people to assimilate, but it conforms more closely to transcendent realities. Avant-garde philosophy is properly an acephalous logic: it labels what is intellectually evident as "prejudice"; seeking to free itself from the servitudes of the mind, it falls into infra-logic; closing itself, above, to the light of the intellect, it opens itself, below, to the darkness of the subconscious.[6] Philosophical skepticism takes itself for an absence of prejudices and a healthy attitude, whereas it is something quite artificial: it is a result not of knowledge but of ignorance, and that is why it is as contrary to intelligence as it is to reality.

The fact that the philosophic mode of thought is centered on logic and not directly on intuition implies that intuition is left at the mercy of logic's needs: in Scholastic disputations it was a question of avoiding certain truths which, given the general level of mentality, might have given rise to certain dangerous conclusions. Scholasticism, it should be remembered, is above all a defense against error: its aim is to be an apologetic and not, as in the case of "metaphysically operative" doctrines — gnosis or *jnāna* — a support for meditation and contemplation. Before Scholasticism, Greek philosophy had also aimed to satisfy a certain need for causal explanations rather than to furnish the intelligence with a means of realization; moreover, the disinterested character of truth easily becomes, on the level of speculative logic, a tendency towards "art for art's sake,"

6. This is what Kant with his rationalistic ingenuousness did not foresee. According to him, every cognition which is not rational in the narrowest sense, is mere pretentiousness and fanciful enthusiasm *(Schwärmerei)*; now, if there is anything pretentious it is this very opinion. Fantasy, arbitrariness and irrationality are not features of the Scholastics, but they certainly are of the rationalists who persist in violently contesting, with ridiculous and often pathetic arguments, everything which eludes their grasp. With Voltaire, Rousseau and Kant, bourgeois (or *vaishya* as the Hindus would say) unintelligence is put forward as a "doctrine" and definitively installed in European "thought," giving birth, by way of the French Revolution, to scientism, industry and to quantitative "culture." Mental hypertrophy in the "cultured" man henceforth compensates the absence of intellectual penetration; the sense of the absolute and the principial is drowned in a mediocre empiricism, coupled with a pseudo-mysticism posing as "positive" or "human." Some people may reproach us with a lack of due consideration, but we would ask what due consideration is shown by philosophers who shamelessly slash down the wisdom of countless centuries.

whence the *ventosa loquacitas philosophorum* stigmatized by Saint Bernard. Some will certainly raise the objection that traditional metaphysics, whether of the East or the West, makes use of rational argumentations like any philosophy; but an argumentation a man uses to describe to his fellow men what he knows is one thing, and an argumentation a man uses on himself because he knows nothing is quite another. This is a capital distinction for it marks the whole difference between the intellectual "visionary" and the mere "thinker" who "gropes alone through the darkness" (Descartes) and whose pride it is to deny that there could be any knowledge which does not proceed in the same fashion.

*
* *

The intellect is a receptive faculty and not a productive power: it does not "create," it receives and transmits; it is a mirror reflecting reality in a manner that is adequate and therefore effective. In most men of the "iron age" the intellect is atrophied to the point of being reduced to a mere virtuality, although doubtless there is no watertight partition between it and the reason, for a sound process of reasoning indirectly transmits something of the intellect; be that as it may, the respective operations of the reason — or the mind — and of the intellect are fundamentally different from the point of view that interests us here, despite certain appearances due to the fact that every man is a thinking being, whether he be wise or ignorant. There is at the same time analogy and opposition: the mind is analogous to the intellect insofar as it is a kind of intelligence, but is opposed to it by its limited, indirect and discursive character; as for the apparent limitations of the intellect, they are merely accidental and extrinsic, while the limits of the mental faculty are inherent in it. Even if the intellect cannot exteriorize the "total truth" — or rather reality — because that is in itself impossible, it can perfectly well establish points of reference which are adequate and sufficient, rather as it is possible to represent space by a circle, a cross, a square, a spiral or a point and so on. Truth and reality must not be confused: the latter relates to "being" and signifies the aseity of things, and the former relates to "knowing" — to the image of reality reflected in the mirror of the intellect — and signifies the adequation of "being" and "knowing"; it is true that reality is often designated by the word "truth," but this is a dialectical synthesis which aims at defining truth in relation to its virtuality of "being," of "reality." If truth is thus made to embrace ontological reality, aseity, the inexpressible, and so also the "personal" realization of the Divine, there is clearly no "total truth" on the plane of thought; but if by "truth" is understood thought insofar as it is an adequate reflection, on the intellectual plane, of "being," there is a "total truth" on this plane, but on condition firstly that nothing quantitative is envisaged in this totality, and secondly that it is made clear that this totality can have a relative sense, according to the order of thought to which it belongs. There is a total truth which is such because it embraces, in principle, all possible truths: this is metaphysical doctrine, whether its enunciation be simple or complex, symbolical or dialectical; but there is also a truth which is total on the plane of spiritual realization, and in this case "truth" becomes synonymous with "reality." Since on the plane of facts there is never anything absolute — or more precisely, nothing "absolutely absolute" — the "totality," while being perfect and sufficient in practice, is always relative in theory; it is indefinitely extensible, but also indefinitely reducible; it can assume the form of an extended doctrine, but also that of a simple sentence, just as the totality of space can be expressed by a system of intertwining patterns too complex for the eye to unravel, but also by an elementary geometrical figure.

We have compared pure intelligence to a mirror; now it must be recalled that there is always a certain element of inversion in the relationship between subject and object, that is, the subject which reflects inverts the object reflected. A tree reflected in water is inverted, and so is "false" in relation to the real tree, but it is still a tree — even "this" tree — and never anything else: consequently the reflected tree is perfectly "true," despite its illusory character, so that it is a mistake to conclude that intellection is illusory because of its subjective framework. The powers of the cosmic illusion are not unlimited, for the Absolute is reflected in the contingent, otherwise the latter would not exist; everything is in God — "All is *Ātmā*" — and the Absolute flashes forth everywhere, it is "infinitely close"; barriers are illusory, they are at the same time immeasurably great and infinitesimally small. The world is antinomic by definition, which is a way of saying it is not God; every image is at the same time true and false, and it suffices to discern the various relationships. Christ is "true God and true man," which is the very formula of the antinomy and parallelism governing the cosmos: antinomy because the creature is not the Creator, and parallelism because nothing can be "outside God," Reality being one.

In a certain sense, doctrine is identical with truth, for account must always be taken of the "relatively absolute"; doctrine should have more than a relative value for us seeing that its content transcends relativities to the extent that it is essential. There is no difficulty in the fact that pure intelligence — the intellect — immensely surpasses thought, and that there is no continuity — despite the identity of essence — between a concept as such and reality, the aseity of the real; to lament over the shortcomings of thought is to ask it to be something that it is not; this is the classical error of philosophers who seek to enclose everything in the *cogito* alone. From the point of view of concrete — not abstract — knowledge of the transcendent, the problem of thought is resolved in the very nature of the intellect.

There are objects which exceed the possibilities of reason; there are none which exceed those of intelligence as such. If there were not something absolute in man — he is "made in the image of God" — he would be only an animal like other animals; but man knows the animals, while they do not know man. Man alone can step out of the cosmos, and this possibility proves — and presupposes — that in a certain way he incarnates the Absolute.[7]

*

* *

If it is useless to seek to establish a "system" embracing every possible aspect of Truth or Reality, it is nonetheless legitimate to develop a traditional perspective to the point of drawing from it all the consequences that human experience can require, and such development will in principle be unlimited. If there can be no exhaustive system of the real, for example, of the intelligible nature of the world, it is because there can be no total coincidence between reality and its reflection in the logical order, otherwise the two would be indistinguishable. However, when there is knowledge of the metaphysical basis from which a given system proceeds, this system can furnish all the keys needed to the reality concerned.

Insofar as the quality of systematization is a perfection, God is systematic — He is a "Geometer" — and so is the truth; but insofar as a system is a limitation, the truth escapes all systematization. Concretely this means that every traditional doctrine has an aspect of system and an aspect of indeterminacy; this latter appears in the variety of orthodox perspectives, hence also in the plurality of systems, such as may appear in the writings of one and the same author, above all in the esoteric field.

In any case it is absurd to want to exploit for the benefit of heterodoxy — and so of freedom of error — scriptural passages like the following: "the Vedas are divided. . . .

7. Without this quality of absoluteness there could be no question either of his salvation or of his damnation.

12

There is no sage whose thought is not divided. . . ." Such texts, far from evincing a more or less agnostic relativism, do no more than state the principle of limitation, of exclusion, of contradiction and division implied in every affirmation. "Why callest thou me good? There is none good but one, that is, God," said Christ; which signifies that every manifestation, even if divine, implies imperfection; it implies it because it is manifestation, and not on account of its content, since the latter may be divine, and therefore "absolute." If a Taoist master could say that "only error is transmitted," it is because there is an inverse relationship between "idea" and "reality," the "thought" and the "lived," the "conceived" and the "realized"; this is the application of the principle which Sufis call "isthmus" *(barzakh)*: seen from above the symbol is darkness, but seen from below, it is light. This inversion, however, is not everything, for there is also direct analogy, essential identity, otherwise there would be no symbolism to provide a framework for the wisdom of the sages; to show the earthly or human side — an inevitable side — of tradition is by no means to destroy tradition.

It was pointed out above that the intellect, which is a mirror, must not be confused with spiritual realization, thanks to which our being, and not merely our thought, participates in the objects which the mirror reflects. The mirror is horizontal, while realization is vertical; the vertical ascent certainly purifies the mirror, but the mirror must adequately reflect the essential outlines of the archetypes, otherwise the ascent is impossible. The goal of spiritual realization cannot go beyond the span of the field of vision, just as in an equilateral triangle the height of the apex depends on the length of the base. Bhaktic doctrine cannot lead as if by chance to the goal envisaged by *jnāna;* an anthropomorphic and individualist "mythology" or a "passional" mysticism excludes a final objective lying beyond the cosmic realm. But the distinction between the intellect and spiritual realization should make us understand above all that if intellectual intuition implies absolute certainty, it does not, however, exclude the possibility of error on a plane of insufficiently known facts, unless these facts fall directly within the "jurisdiction" of the intellectual mode in question; this question has already been referred to in connection with authority. Every manifestation of absoluteness — and the authority flowing from intellectual intuition is one such — presupposes an appropriate framework: "the perfect man" — said a Buddhist master — "may be uninformed on secondary matters of which he has no experience, but he can never be wrong on what his power of discernment has already revealed to him. . . . He knows clay, but he has not acquired knowledge of every form that clay can be given." On the other hand it must not be forgotten that, as was mentioned above, intellectual intuition may operate only within certain "dimensions" of the spirit, according to given modes or within given domains; the intelligence may be centered on some particular aspect of the real. The drawbacks which may result from such differences are however neutralized, in the broadest sense, by the traditional framework, which offers to each predisposition its appropriate field.

*
* *

Man — insofar as he is distinct from other creatures on earth — is intelligence; and intelligence — in its principle and its plenitude — is knowledge of the Absolute; the Absolute is the fundamental content of the intelligence and determines its nature and functions. What distinguishes man from animals is not knowledge of a tree, but the concept — whether explicit or implicit — of the Absolute; it is from this that the whole hierarchy of values is derived, and hence all notion of a homogeneous world. God is the "motionless mover" of every operation of the mind, even when man — reason — makes himself out to be the measure of God.

14

To say that man is the measure of all things is meaningless unless one starts from the idea that God is the measure of man, or that the absolute is the measure of the relative, or again, that the universal Intellect is the measure of individual existence; nothing is fully human that is not determined by the Divine, and therefore centered on it. Once man makes of himself a measure, while refusing to be measured in turn, or once he makes definitions while refusing to be defined by what transcends him and gives him all his meaning, all human reference points disappear; cut off from the Divine, the human collapses.

In our times it is the machine which tends to become the measure of man, and thereby it becomes something like the measure of God, though of course in a diabolically illusory manner; for the most "advanced" minds it is in fact the machine, technics, experimental science, which will henceforth dictate to man his nature, and it is these which create the truth — as is shamelessly admitted — or rather what usurps its place in man's consciousness. It is difficult for man to fall lower, to realize a greater mental perversion, a more complete abandonment of himself, a more perfect betrayal of his intelligent and free personality: in the name of "science" and of "human genius" man consents to become the creation of what he has created and to forget what he is, to the point of expecting the answer to this from machines and from the blind forces of nature; he has waited until he is no longer anything and now claims to be his own creator. Swept away by a torrent, he glories in his incapacity to resist it.

And just as matter and machines are quantitative, so man too becomes quantitative: the human is henceforth the social. It is forgotten that man, by isolating himself, can cease to be social, whereas society, whatever it may do — and it is in fact incapable of acting of itself — can never cease to be human.

15

*

*   *

Transcendent knowledge — provided it is real, that is to say "visionary" and not simply "dialectical" — is deepened by asceticism, for asceticism contributes in its own way to the transition from "knowing" to "being," from theory to realization, just as ascesis is in turn deepened by knowledge, where this latter is within the possibilities of the man; but when it is not so, ascesis has no power to produce gnosis — or rather to be the condition of its blossoming — for no discipline can modify the scope of the human receptacle, although it can doubtless produce, in the course of spiritual development, transmutations that seem miraculous. It is obviously absurd to evaluate some ascetic practice in terms of its possible fruits in respect of sacred knowledge, for that would oblige one to question the heroic qualities of many saints. And conversely, it is just as illogical to make this knowledge depend on conditions of will or morality which are comparatively external, for knowledge alone implies intrinsic certainty, that is to say it imposes itself by its very nature of intelligibility and self-evidence, and not by contingent conditions. This could also be expressed as follows: if knowledge is a grace, it is a free gift, and if it is freely given, it could not depend essentially on attitudes of will, otherwise it would be necessary to conclude that grace is their product; or again, if knowledge cannot depend, subjectively, on an extrinsic condition such as ascetic effort, truth in its turn cannot depend, objectively, on an extrinsic condition such as its attachment to a subjective phenomenon, namely the ascetic perfection of a particular individual. Moreover, if on the one hand it be admitted that ascesis is a preparation for grace — in the sense of a logical condition and not of an efficient cause — it must on the other hand be understood that metaphysical intellection, which is direct and therefore "concrete," implies a certain detachment with regard to the world and the "I," and demands a posteriori an ascesis conforming to its nature.

Man can, in a certain sense,[8] will what God does not will; but he cannot in any sense know what God does not know. Vice always comes from the will, but error as such never comes from knowledge; hence there is in the intellect an element of participation or union with God, a supernatural and not simply human element, and this marks in an eminently qualitative way a clear distinction between knowledge and will. To say that the intellect can "penetrate" the divine mysteries — and it can do so for the simple reason that it bears traces of them in its very substance — does not mean that it can "exhaust" them, for God is infinite, and the mirror is not the object it reflects. In reality, it is not the intellect which penetrates God, but God who penetrates the intellect; no one can choose God who has not been chosen by Him.

*

* *

We cannot insist too strongly on the following: if the relative did not comprise something of the absolute, relativities could not be distinguished qualitatively from one another. It is clearly not as a relativity that orthodoxy gives salvation, but by virtue of its quality of absoluteness. Revelation is infallible light insofar as it is the divine Subject objectified, but not insofar as it is objectification pure and simple. Revelation, tradition, orthodoxy and intellectual intuition would be inconceivable but for the qualitative and quasi-absolute element which is present at the center and

---

8. "In a certain sense" for, if it be true that God does not desire sin, there is, in the last analysis, nothing that takes place outside the divine Will. God "wills evil" insofar as the latter is a necessary element in the cosmic equilibrium; to cut off evil from the world would mean to abolish the world.

17

in the arteries of the cosmos, and which flashes forth to produce the phenomenon of the sacred.

The Vedanta

Among explicit doctrines, the Vedanta stands out as one of the most direct formulations possible of what constitutes the very essence of our spiritual reality. This directness is compensated by its requirement of renunciation, or, more precisely, of total detachment *(vairāgya)*.

The Vedantic perspective finds its equivalents in the great religions which regulate humanity, for truth is one. Their formulation, however, may be dependent on dogmatic perspectives which restrict their immediate intelligibility, or which make direct expressions of them difficult of access. In fact, whereas Hinduism is as it were made up of autonomous parts, the monotheistic religions are organisms in which the various parts are formally bound up with the whole.

Hinduism, although it is organically linked with the Upanishads, is nevertheless not reducible to the Shivaite Vedantism of Shankara, although this must be considered as the essence of the Vedanta and so of the Hindu tradition.

*
* *

The Vedanta of Shankara, which is here more particularly being considered, is Divine and immemorial in its origin and in no sense the creation of Shankara, who was only its great and providential spokesman. It has in view above all the mental virtues, those which converge towards perfect and permanent concentration, whereas moralities — whether Hindu or Monotheist — extend the same principles to the domain of action, which is almost suppressed in the case of the wandering monk (or *sannyāsi*). Thus, calmness of mind *(shama)* becomes, in the case of the Moslem, for example, contentment *(ridhā)* or trust in God *(tawakkul)*, which in fact produces calmness of mind. The Vedanta retains the alchemical essence of the virtues.[1]

*
* *

According to the Vedanta, the contemplative must become absolutely "Himself"; according to other perspectives such as that of the Semitic religions, man must become absolutely "Other" than himself — or than the "I" — which from the point of view of pure truth amounts to exactly the same thing.

*
* *

In Sufism the term *Huwa*, "He," in no way signifies that the Divine Aseity is conceived in an objectified mode, but solely that it is beyond the distinction between subject and object which is designated by the terms *anā* and *anta*, "I-thou."

The Divine Subject, by descending into the plane of cosmic objectification, illuminates it by virtue of the mystery of the Spirit, *Ar-Rūh*, and sustains — and also absorbs — this plane by virtue of the mystery of the "Light," *An-Nūr.*

---

1. This is what Ibn Al-Arif also does when he seems to reject, one after another, the religious virtues. In reality he detaches them both from the self-interested ego and from the anthropomorphic aspect of the Divinity, in order to keep only their essences. It is to be noted that Hinduism also knows contentment *(santosha)* and trust in God *(prapatti)*, but the *sannyāsi* goes beyond them.

*

*   *

The demiurgic tendency is conceived in the Vedanta as an objectification, and in Sufism it is conceived as an individuation, and so in fact as a subjectification, God being then, not pure Subject as in the Hindu perspective, but pure Object, "He" *(Huwa),* That which no subjective vision limits. This divergence lies only in the form, for it goes without saying that the "Subject" of the Vedanta is anything but an individual determination and that the Sufic "Object" is anything but the effect of an ignorance. The Self *(Ātmā)* is "He," for it is "purely objective" in as much as it excludes all individuation and the "He" *(Huwa)* is "Self" and so "purely subjective" in the sense that it excludes all objectification.

The Sufic formula *Lā anā wa lā Anta: Huwa* (Neither I nor Thou: He) is thus equivalent to the formula of the Upanishads *Tat tvam asi* (That art thou).

*

*   *

Where the Vedantist speaks of the "unicity of the Subject" (or more precisely non-duality, *advaita),* a Sufi will speak of the "unicity of Existence" (that is, of Reality, *waḥdat al-Wujūd).* In Hindu terms the difference is that the Vedantist insists on the aspect of *Chit* (Consciousness) and the Sufi on the aspect of *Sat* (Being).[2]

2. At least in the school of *Wujūdiyah* (from *Wujūd,* Existence, *Wujūd muṭlaq* being Absolute Existence, God) though not in that of *Shuhūdiyah* (from *shuhūd,* direct vision, the word *Shāhid* meaning "Witness" like the Sanskrit word *Sākshin)* the perspective of which is closely analogous to that of the Vedanta. The two perspectives referred to necessarily have a Koranic foundation, but the former is doubtless more in conformity with the most apparent meaning of the Book. The latter school has been falsely accused of immanentism because of its thesis of the "One Witness" and of indefinitely diversified "mirrors."

That which in man goes beyond individuality and all separateness is not only pure Consciousness but also pure Existence. Ascesis purifies the existential side of man and thus indirectly purifies the intellectual side.

If man could confine himself to "being" he would be holy by that very fact; this is what quietism believed it had understood.

*

* *

Ātmā is pure Light and Beatitude, pure Consciousness, pure Subject.[3] There is nothing unrelated to this Reality; even the "object" which is least in conformity with It is still It, but "objectified" by *Māyā*, the power of illusion consequent upon the infinity of the Self.

This is the very definition of universal objectification. But within it one must distinguish further between two fundamental modes, one subjective and the other objective. The first mode is the following: between the object as such and the pure and infinite Subject there stands, as it were, the objectified Subject, that is to say the cognitive act through which, by analysis and synthesis, the bare object is brought back to the Subject. This function of objectifying (in relation to the Subject, which then, as it were, projects itself upon the objective plane), or of subjectifying (in relation to the object which is integrated in the subjective and so brought back to the Divine Subject), is the spirit which knows and discerns, the manifested intelligence, the

3. The notion of "the subject," far from being only psychological, is before all else logical and principial and so cannot be restricted to any particular domain; the obvious subjectivity of the faculties of sensation already proves that the pair "subject-object" does not belong solely to the realm of psychology. All the more is it true that metaphysical notions such as the Witness *(Sākshin)* in the Vedanta or, in Sufism, the Knower *(Al-'Aqil,* with its complement *Al-Ma'qūl,* the Known), or again the Divine Subjectivity *(Anniyah,* with its complement *Huwiyah,* the Divine Objectivity) have nothing whatever to do with any kind of psychology.

consciousness, which is relative and so capable in its turn of being an object of knowledge.

The other fundamental mode of objectification may be described thus: in order to realize the Subject, which is *Sat* (Being), *Chit* (Knowledge or Consciousness) and *Ānanda* (Beatitude), one must know that objects are superimposed upon the Subject and concentrate one's mind on the Subject alone. Between the objective world, which then becomes identified with ignorance *(avidyā)* and the Subject, the Self *(Ātmā)*, there is interposed an objectification of the Subject. This objectification is direct and central; it is revelation, truth, grace and therefore it is also the *Avatāra,* the *guru,* the doctrine, the method, the *mantra.*

Thus the sacred formula, the *mantra,* symbolizes and incarnates the Subject by objectifying It and, by "covering" the objective world, this dark cavern of ignorance, or rather by "substituting" itself for it, the *mantra* leads the spirit lost in the labyrinth of objectification back to the pure Subject.

That is why in the most diverse traditions, the *mantra* and its practice, *japa,* are referred to as recollection (the *dhikr* of Sufism): with the aid of the symbol, of the Divine Name, the spirit which has gone astray and become separated recollects that it is pure Consciousness, pure Subject, pure Self.

*

* *

That the Real and the unreal are "not different" does not in any way imply either the unreality of the Self or the reality of the world. To start with, the Real is not "non-different" with respect to the unreal; it is the unreal which is non-different with respect to the Real, not, that is, inasmuch as it is unreality, but inasmuch as it is a "lesser reality," the latter being nonetheless "extrinsically unreal" in relation to Absolute Reality.

*

*   *

Māyā, illusion or the "Divine Art"[4] which expresses *Ātmā* according to indefinitely varied modes — and of which *avidyā,* the ignorance which conceals *Ātmā,* is the purely negative aspect — proceeds mysteriously from *Ātmā* Itself, in the sense that *Māyā* is a necessary consequence of *Ātmā's* infinity. Shankaracharya expresses this by saying that *Māyā* is without beginning.

Ātma is beyond the opposition of subject-object; one can, however, call it pure Subject when one starts from the consideration of "objects," which are so many superimpositions in relation to *Ātmā.*

Māyā is the objectifying (or manifesting) tendency. The principal degrees of objectification (or manifestation) are the "feet" *(pādas)* of *Ātmā* or, from the standpoint of the hierarchy of microcosmic states, its envelopes *(koshas).* Each degree of objectification is equivalent to a more or less indirect image of *Ātmā,* an image reflected inversely; at the same time, each degree realizes an inversion in relation to the one which is above it and by which it is contained, because the relationship of Subject-objectification (or Principle-manifestation) is repeated from one *pāda* or *kosha* to another; thus the animic or subtle objectification is principial in relation to the corporal or gross objectification, and likewise the supra-formal objectification is principial in relation to the formal objectification, which for its part contains both the animic and corporal planes. However, the universal and fundamental inversion as between Subject and objectification is never done away with as a result of the inversions comprised within the objectification itself, for these are never produced under the same relationship and never under any relationship capable of nullifying that first

4. Ananda K. Coomaraswamy suggested the word "art" as a translation of *Māyā* to show its positive function.

inversion. Inversion *within* an inversion is therefore never inversion *of* the inversion, never, that is to say, a re-establishment of the "normal" relationship. In other words, the subordinate inversion which, within the great inversion represented by the Cosmos in relation to the Self, appears as if it ought to nullify the latter — since it inverts it symbolically — is in its turn inverse in relation to the Divine Norm. An opaque body does not become transparent when painted white to compensate for its opacity, although the color white represents light or transparency, and for that reason also represents the negation of the opacity; or again, the fact that a body is black adds nothing to its opacity.[5] Therefore, if formal manifestation — both subtle and gross — is inverse in relation to formless manifestation, this nevertheless does not cancel the inversion realized by formless manifestation in relation to non-manifestation — or non-objectification — which is the Self, the Subject.

*

*   *

It is very easy to label as "vague" and "contradictory" something which through lack of "intellectual vision" one cannot understand. Rationalist thinkers generally refuse to admit a truth that presents contradictory aspects and that is situated, seemingly beyond grasping, midway between two extrinsic and negative enunciations. Now there are some realities which could be formulated in no other way

---

5. When Sufism teaches that the trees of Paradise have their roots above, it would be wrong to try to grasp this idea by means of the imagination, for the relation in question, once it is translated into terrestrial forms, is expressed, precisely, by the terrestrial position of trees. In other words, if one were to behold the trees of Paradise, a spirit endowed with the appropriate faculty of vision would accept them as being "normal," exactly in the same way as the mind accepts the trees on this earth. In this order of ideas it is instructive to note the fact that the retina of the eye receives only inverted images and that it is the mind which re-establishes the normal and objective relationship.

than this. The ray which proceeds from a light is itself light, since it illumines, but it is not the light from which it proceeds; therefore it is neither that light nor yet other than that light; in point of fact it is nothing else but light, though growing ever weaker in proportion to its distance from its source. A faint glow is light for the darkness it illumincs, but darkness for the light whence it emanates. Similarly *Māyā* is both light and darkness at the same time: She is light[6] inasmuch as, being the Divine art, she reveals the secrets of *Ātmā*. As darkness she is ignorance, *avidyā.*[7]

*
* *

In spiritual realization the cosmic tendency of objectification is captured by the Symbol: in the natural course of its drawing away from *Ātmā* the soul meets the objectification, in this case direct and not indirect, of the pure Subject; the indirect objectification is the world with its endless diversity, and the direct objectification is the Symbol, which replaces the pure Subject on the objectified plane. *Ātmā* resides in the center of man as "Subject," pure and infinite, and it surrounds man as the indefinitely differentiated objectification of this "Subject." The yogi or *mukta,* the "delivered one," perceives *Ātmā* in everything, but the man who is undelivered has to superimpose on the world the synthetic and direct image of *Ātmā* in order to eliminate the superimposition in relation to *Ātmā* which the world itself represents. A symbol is anything that serves as a direct

6. "*Māyā*, by the very fact that she is the 'Divine art' inherent in the Principle, is also identified with Wisdom *(Sophia)* understood in precisely the same sense as is given to it in the Judaeo-Christian tradition; as such she is the mother of the *Avatāra*" (René Guénon: "*Māyā,*" in *Etudes Traditionelles,* July-August, 1947). This is what Islamic esoterism designates by the terms "Science" *('Ilm)* and "Light" *(Nūr).*
7. To this "ignorance" there corresponds, in Islamic terminology, "association" *(shirk),* that is to say the fact of associating a "superimposition" with Unity.

support for spiritual realization, as, for example, a *mantra* or a Divine name, or, in a secondary way, a graphic, pictorial or sculptured symbol such as a sacred image *(pratīka)*.

*

* *

The revelation of Sinai, the Messianic redemption, the descent of the Koran — these are so many examples of the Subjectifying objectification effected by the symbol, in which *Ātmā* is incarnated in *Māyā* and *Māyā* expresses *Ātmā*.

*

* *

To say, as do the Vedantists, that *Māyā* is an attribute of *Īshvara* and that *Māyā* expresses *Īshvara* and at the same time veils Him, signifies clearly that the world derives from the infinity of *Ātmā*. One could also say that the world is a consequence of the absolute necessity of Being.

*

* *

If *Māyā* is presented as a postulate, this must not be understood in a philosophical or psychological sense as if it were a question of a hypothesis, for this postulate is necessary and consequently corresponds to an objective reality. *Māyā*, taken as the purely negative factor of objectification, cannot possibly be known positively; she therefore imprints herself on the intelligence as an unextended and ungraspable element.

In a certain sense *Māyā* represents the possibility for Being of not being. The All-Possibility must by definition and on pain of contradiction include its own impossibility.

It is in order not to be, that Being incarnates in the multitude of souls; it is in order not to be, that the ocean squanders itself in myriad flecks of foam.

If the soul obtains deliverance, that is because Being is.

*
* *

Nothing is external to absolute Reality; the world is therefore a kind of internal dimension of *Brahma*. But *Brahma* is without relativity; thus the world is a necessary aspect of the absolute necessity of *Brahma*. Put in another way, relativity is an aspect of the Absolute.

Relativity, *Māyā*, is the *Shakti* of the Absolute, *Brahma*.

If the relative did not exist, the Absolute would not be the Absolute.

*
* *

The essence of the world, which is diversity, is *Brahma*. It might be objected that *Brahma* cannot be the essence of a diversity since It is non-duality. To be sure, *Brahma* is not the essence of the world, for, from the standpoint of the Absolute, the world does not exist; but one can say that the world, insofar as it does exist, has *Brahma* for its essence; otherwise it would possess no reality whatsoever. Diversity, for its part, is but the inverse reflection of the Infinity, or of the all-possibility, of *Brahma*.

*
* *

Natural things are the indirect objectifications of the Self; the supernatural is Its direct and flashing objectification.

The Cosmos is the total objectification, "made in the image of God," which includes all other cosmic objectifications.

The cosmic objectification of the Self presupposes the Divine Objectification, Being, *Īshvara,* or *Apara-Brahma.* Sufism expresses it by this formula, "I was a hidden treasure and I wished to be known."

*

* *

Union *(yoga)*: the Subject *(Ātmā)* becomes object (the Veda, the *Dharma)* so that the object (the objectified subject, man) may become the (absolute) Subject.

Deification: God became man so that man might become God. Man pre-exists in God — this is the "Son" — and God pre-exists in man — this is the Intellect. The point of contact between God and man is, objectively, Christ and, subjectively it is the purified heart, "intelligence-love."

Unification *(tawḥīd): the One *(illā 'Llāh)* became naught *(lā ilāha)*, in order that the naught might become the One; the One became separate and multiple (the Koran) in order that the separate and multiple (the soul) might become the One. The "multiple" pre-exists in the One — this is the uncreate Koran, the eternal Word — and the "One" pre-exists in the multiple: this is the heart-intellect, and in the macrocosm it is the universal Spirit.

*

* *

The conceptions of Ramanuja are contained in those of Shankara and are transcended by them. When Shankara sees in the localization and duration of sensory objects a direct and tangible manifestation of their unreality, he does not say, as Ramanuja seems to have believed, that they do not exist as objects, but he says that as existing objects they are unreal. Ramanuja affirms against Shankaracharya truths which the latter never denied on their own level. Ramanuja shows a tendency to put everything in a concrete form as a function of the created world, and this indeed corresponds both with the Vishnuite point of view and with the Western outlook which shares the same perspective.

*

* *

The antagonism between Shankara and Nagarjuna is of the same order as that which opposes Ramanuja to Shankara, with this difference, however, that, if Shankara rejects the doctrine of Nagarjuna, it is because the form of the latter corresponds — independently of its real content and of the spiritual virtuality it represents — to a more restricted perspective than that of the Vedanta. When, on the other hand, Ramanuja rejects the doctrine of Shankara it is for the opposite reason. The perspective of Shankara goes beyond that of Ramanuja, not merely in respect of its form, but in respect of its very basis.

In order really to understand Nagarjuna, or the Mahayana in general, one must before everything else take account of two facts, first that Buddhism presents itself essentially as a spiritual method and so subordinates everything to the point of view of method and, secondly, that this method is essentially one of negation. From this it follows, on the one hand, that metaphysical reality is considered with reference to method, that is as "state" and not as "principle," and, on the other hand, that it is conceived in negative terms: *Nirvāna,* Extinction, or *Shūnya,* the Void. In Buddhist wisdom, affirmation has the same meaning and function as subjectivism, and hence ignorance, in Hindu wisdom. To describe *Nirvāna* or *Shūnya* in positive terms would amount, in Vedantine language, to wishing to know the pure Subject, the Divine Consciousness, *Ātmā,* on the plane of objectification itself, hence on the plane of ignorance.

*

* *

When Westerners refer to something as being "positive" they almost always think of manifestation, of the created; hence their preference for the perspective of Ramanuja and their mistake in attributing "abstractions" to Shankara — or to Plato.

God is abstraction for the world because the world is abstraction in relation to God.[8] Now it is God who is real, not the world.

*
* *

People often believe that the content of a statement is false to the extent that the enunciation can be attacked by dialectics. Now every statement the content of which is not a fact that can be checked physically or rationally, that is every transcendent truth, can be contradicted by arguments drawn from experience. Shankara never said that the inevitably human formulation of truth, bearing for instance on absolute Consciousness, could not be attacked; he said that such formulations were intrinsically true and something that the reason alone could not verify. When the *Advaitins* say that Consciousness has such and such a nature and that the example of deep sleep shows it, that does not at all mean that they themselves had need of this example or that they could be discomfited by a demonstration of the gaps it necessarily contains. Clearly it is not because of a contrary aspect but because of an analogy that one has recourse to an example. Contrary aspects do exist but they are not relevant here. If we say that, compared to an opaque body, any light is like the sun, the fact that this light has neither the form, nor the dimensions, nor the matter of the sun is absolutely without significance in this connection; moreover, if the example differed in no way from the thing to be demonstrated, it would be, not an example, but the thing itself.

8. It should be noted here that the word "God" does not and cannot admit of any restriction for the simple reason that God is "all that is purely principial" and that He is thus also — and a fortiori — Beyond-Being; this one may not know or may deny, but one cannot deny that God is "That which is supreme" and therefore also That which nothing can surpass.

*

* *

Intellectual intuition communicates a priori the reality of the Absolute.

Reasoning thought infers the Absolute by starting from the relative; thus it does not proceed by intellectual intuition, though it does not inevitably exclude it.

For philosophy, arguments have an absolute value; for intellectual intuition their value is symbolical and provisional.

Shankara did not "construct a system";[9] he did not "seek a solution" of such and such a "problem." He did not suffer from what he himself calls the disease of doubt.

Shankara is like a colorless glass which allows the rays of light to pass through it intact whereas Ramanuja might be compared to a colored glass which also transmits light, but imparts to it a certain tint; this is to say that Ramanuja's doctrine also is inspired and not invented. Sages are instruments for the crystallizing of the pure Light; they are anything but inventors of systems. It is intellection that determines everything; the mode of expression is dictated by the requirements of the particular traditional form. With philosophers in the ordinary meaning of the word the initiative comes from the human side, from mental restlessness, from doubt, from lack of contemplative quality; their attitude is Promethean, not prophetic.

*

* *

9. By this is meant an assemblage of concordant reasonings hierarchically arranged. It is true that one can always describe an orthodox doctrine as a "system" when comparing it to some system in nature, such as the solar system; in fact a doctrine is in the nature of things, an assemblage of ideas grouped harmoniously round a central idea from which they derive according to various "dimensions."

God cannot change; therefore He cannot be the cause of change as such. He is the cause of all things, and He is consequently the cause of what appears to us as change; but He is its cause not inasmuch as it is change, but inasmuch as this apparent change, which for us is real, affirms an aspect of the Immutable. Or again, simply to consider change as such, God is its cause only inasmuch as the change, or all change, expresses in the language of diversity the Divine infinity or all-possibility.

The world, inasmuch as it is subject to change, cannot have God for its cause; from the standpoint of its negative character the world is not. On the other hand, change insofar as it expresses infinity — not insofar as it negates immutability — must have God for its cause, and in this respect the world exists, even though in the last analysis it is reducible to that cause itself. An effect, to the extent that it is ontologically positive, is not really distinct from its cause.

*
* *

It has sometimes been argued that the delivered sage, the *vidwān,* having attained the state whence there is no return (into the karmic chain of samsaric existences), has passed beyond our ken and can consequently no longer speak or teach. Now the *Advaitins* have never denied the double nature of the *vidwān.* If Christianity were not the religion of the West and if the twofold nature of Christ were not a dogma, no doubt the same philosophers who seek for contradictions in the Vedanta would declare the two natures of Christ to be incompatible and would describe this dogma as a "stumbling block"; they would do the same as regards the Trinity.

*
* *

It is contradictory to maintain — in order to contest the reality of the absolute Subject — that the intellective light is real only in respect of its projection on an external object and that it thus has only a relative and extrinsic reality. A contrast can reveal the nature of something or bring out its value, but it cannot create that nature; it could not reveal a nature that did not exist. God is Light in Himself and not because He illuminates our darkness. On the contrary, He illuminates the darkness because He is Light in Itself: He is Love, not because He loves, but He loves because He is Love.

*

* *

There is between the soul and *Brahma* both continuity and discontinuity at the same time, depending on the standpoint from which the relationship is viewed: continuity from the point of view of the essential nature, which is consciousness, and discontinuity from the point of view of the "actual nature," which is pure Consciousness on the Divine side, and objectified consciousness on the human side — objectified in its very cosmic root and consequently darkened, limited and divided by *avidyā,* by ignorance. Hence it follows that the individual substance, even when empirically emptied of its objective content, is by no means freed thereby from the fundamental vice of objectification, which can only be eliminated by Knowledge.

The being as such, that is to say considered as a mode of objectification, necessarily envisages the single Consciousness — from which in reality he is not distinct — as external. The *Avatāras* adored God concurrently with their state of "identity" and on another plane, and therefore "outside" themselves.

The great defect of the soul — the "original sin" — is not the accidental objectification which causes a being to be distracted by one object or another, but rather the fundamental objectification which makes this possible. Now the

34

fundamental objectification is collective and hereditary; it belongs to the species, and not to the will of the individual.

Pseudo-Vedantist subjectivism — which in reality is solipsism — is incapable of taking account of the objective homogeneity of the cosmic environment.

*

* *

It is *Ātmā* objectified as *jīvātmā* or *ahankāra* which is the subject of mental objectification; it is thus a subject already objectified, secondary and relative.

When the individual empties his mind of all objects he approaches *Ātmā* in a certain symbolical way, but the objectification represented by the individual as such is not thereby abolished — far from it. Spiritual realization is neither solipsism nor auto-suggestion.

*

* *

Christ could say, "Why callest thou me good? There is none good but one, that is God." This signifies that everything necessarily participates in the essential attributes of relativity.

Shankaracharya used such expressions as this: "I prostrate myself before *Govinda* whose nature is supreme Bliss." And Ramakrishna said, "In the Absolute I am not and you are not and God (as Personal God) is not, for the Absolute is beyond all speech and thought. But so long as there still exists something outside myself, I must adore Brahma within the limits of my mind as something which is outside me."

*

* *

Direct analogy and inverse analogy; in the former case a tree reflected in water will never be anything but a tree, in the latter the reflected tree will always be upside down.

Between God and the world, between the Principle and manifestation, between the Uncreate and the created there is always — but in different respects — both direct analogy and inverse analogy. Thus the ego is not only a reflection but also a negation of the Self; God can consequently be called the "Divine I" by analogy with what is positive, conscious and immortal in the human "I," but He can also be called "He" in opposition to the negative, ignorant and unreal aspects of the human "I." The term "the Self" expresses both the analogy and the opposition.

*

* *

To say that Reality can never be attained by one who maintains the objective illusion is to forget that union depends, not on some particular terminology, but on the fusion of two distinct elements, whether we call these "subject" and "object" or something else; it amounts in any case to replacing the objective illusion, which is normal since it is general, by a subjective illusion, which is abnormal and therefore far more dangerous. In order to be united to something it is by no means necessary to start by pretending that one is not separate from it in any way or in any respect, or, in short, that one does not exist; one must not replace intellection by a facile and blind conviction.

*

* *

It is useless to seek to realize that "I am *Brahma*" before understanding that "I am not *Brahma*"; it is useless to seek to realize that "*Brahma* is my true Self" before understanding that "*Brahma*" is outside me; it is useless to seek to realize that "*Brahma* is pure Consciousness" before understanding that "*Brahma* is the Almighty Creator."[10]

10. "No man cometh unto the Father but by me." The following *ḥadīth* bears the same meaning: "He who desires to meet Allah must first meet His Prophet."

*

*   *

It is not possible to understand that the enunciation "I am not *Brahma*" is false before having understood that it is true. Similarly it is not possible to understand that the enunciation "*Brahma* is outside me" is not exact before having understood that it is; and similarly again, it is not possible to understand that the enunciation "*Brahma* is the Almighty Creator" contains an error before having understood that it expresses a truth.

*

*   *

If, in order to be able to speak of the Self, one must have realized the Self, how can one who has not realized it know that one must have realized it in order to be able to speak of it? If some sage can alone know what the Self is, because he has himself realized it, how can his disciples know he has realized it and that he alone knows what the Self is?

Under these conditions there would remain only absolute ignorance face to face with absolute knowledge, and there would be no possible contact with the Self, no spiritual realization and no difference between the intelligent man and the fool, or between truth and error. To attribute to knowledge a purely subjective and empirical background which is at the same time absolute amounts to the very negation of intellect, and consequently of intellection; it is also a negation of inspiration and of revelation. In other words it amounts to a denial, first, of intelligence, then of its illumination by the Self and, finally, of the Prophetic and Law-giving manifestation of the Self in a given world. It therefore means the destruction of tradition, for in these conditions the unicity and permanence of the Veda would remain inexplicable. Every realized being would write a new Veda and found a new religion; the *Sanātana Dharma* would be a concept devoid of meaning.

*

*   *

Intellection, inspiration, revelation. These three realities are essential for man and for the human collectivity. They are distinct one from another, but none can be reduced simply to a question of realization. The realized man can have inspirations that are — as to their production — distinct from his state of knowledge,[11] but he could not add one syllable to the Veda. Moreover inspirations may depend on a spiritual function, for instance on that of a pontiff,[12] just as they may also result from a mystical degree. As for revelation, it is quite clear that the most perfect spiritual realization could not bring it about, although such realization is its *conditio sine qua non*.

As for intellection, it is an essential condition of the realization in question, for it alone can give to the human initiative its sufficient reason and its efficacy. This fundamental role of pure intelligence is an aspect of "becoming what one is."

Revelation is in a certain sense the intellection of the collectivity, or rather it takes the place of that. For the collectivity as such it is the only way of knowing, and it is for this reason that the *Avatāra* through whom the revelation is brought about must, in his normalizing perfection, incarnate the humanity which he both represents and enlightens.

This is why the prayer of a saint is always a prayer of all and for all.

---

11. There are very many instances of this: thus Shri Ramana Maharshi said that his stanzas (*Ulladu Narpadu* or *Sad-Vidya*) came to him as if "from outside." And he even described how they became fixed in his mind without the collaboration of his will.

12. This is directly connected with "grace of state" (the grace attaching to a function), "authority," "infallibility" and the "help of the Holy Spirit."

*

*   *

To believe, with certain neo-yogists, that evolution will produce a superman "who will differ from man as much as man differs from the animal or the animal from the vegetable" is a case of not knowing what man is. Here is one more example of a pseudo-wisdom which deems itself vastly superior to the "separatist" religions, but which in point of fact shows itself more ignorant than the most elementary of catechisms. For the most elementary catechism does know what man is: it knows that by his qualities, and as an autonomous world, he stands opposed to the other kingdoms of nature taken together; it knows that in one particular respect — that of spiritual possibilities, not that of animal nature — the difference between a monkey and a man is infinitely greater than that between a fly and a monkey. For man alone is able to leave the world; man alone is able to return to God; and that is the reason why he cannot in any way be surpassed by a new earthly being. Among the beings of this earth man is the central being; this is an absolute position; there cannot be a center more central than the center, if definitions have any meaning.

This neo-yogism, like other similar movements, pretends that it can add an essential value to the wisdom of our ancestors; it believes that the religions are partial truths which it is called upon to put together, after hundreds or thousands of years of waiting, and to crown with its own naive little system.

*

*   *

It is far better to believe that the earth is a disk supported by a tortoise and flanked by four elephants than to believe, in the name of evolution, in the coming of some superhuman monster.

A literal interpretation of cosmological symbols is, if not positively useful, at any rate harmless, whereas a scientific error — such as evolutionism — is neither literally nor symbolically true; the repercussions of its falsity are incalculable.

*
*   *

The intellectual poverty of the neo-yogist movement provides an incontestable proof that there is no spirituality without orthodoxy. It is assuredly not by chance that all these movements are as if in league against the intelligence; intelligence is replaced by a thinking that is feeble and vague instead of being logical, and "dynamic" instead of being contemplative. All these movements are characterized by an affectation of detachment in regard to pure doctrine. They hate its incorruptibility, for in their eyes this purity is "dogmatism"; they fail to understand that Truth does not deny forms from the outside, but transcends them from within.

Orthodoxy includes and guarantees infinitely precious values which man could not possibly draw out of himself.

*
*   *

In Shri Ramana Maharshi one meets again ancient and eternal India. The Vedantic truth — the truth of the Upanishads — is brought back to its simplest expression but without any kind of betrayal. It is the simplicity inherent in the Real, not the denial of that complexity which it likewise contains, nor the artificial and altogether outward simplification that springs from ignorance.

That spiritual function which can be described as "action of presence" found in the Maharshi its most rigorous expression. Shri Ramana was as it were the incarnation, in these latter days and in the face of the modern activist fever, of what is primordial and incorruptible in India. He manifested the nobility of contemplative non-action in the face of an ethic of utilitarian agitation, and he showed the implacable beauty of pure truth in the face of passions, weaknesses and betrayals.

The great question "Who am I?" appears, with him, as a concrete expression of a reality that is lived, if one may so put it, and this authenticity gives to each word of the sage a flavor of inimitable freshness — the flavor of Truth when it is embodied in the most immediate way.

The whole Vedanta is contained in the Maharshi's question "Who am I"? The answer is: the Inexpressible.

A View of Yoga

Yoga is the most direct and also the most ample manifestation possible of a spiritual principle which, as such, must be able to reveal itself whenever the nature of things permits or demands it: this principle is essentially that of a technique — or an "alchemy" — designed to open the human microcosm to the divine influx. Yoga itself is defined as a "cessation of the activities of the mental substance," and strictly speaking there is only one Yoga — the art of perfect concentration, of which *Hatha-Yoga* and *Raja-Yoga* are the two essential forms, and of which the other Yogas *(Laya* and *Mantra)* are special modalities or developments. It is true that the word Yoga also designates — in virtue of its literal sense of "Union" — the three great paths of gnosis *(jnāna),* love *(bhakti)* and action *(karma);* but the connection with the principle that characterizes the yogic art is then much less direct. Yoga, as defined in the *Sūtras* of Patanjali and related works, is always the interior alchemy, or the ensemble of technical means for realizing — with the aid of intellectual, corporal, moral and sometimes emotional elements — union through ecstasy or *samādhi.*[1]

1. The word "ecstasy" can include several meanings, depending on the mode or degree of rapture; but in every case it indicates a departure from terrestrial consciousness, whether this departure be active or passive in character, or rather, whatever may be the combination of these two characteristics.

The following example will serve to clarify the distinction just established — though admittedly too schematic, it is nonetheless instructive: with *jnāna*, "humility" is awareness of the nothingness of the ego considered from the standpoint of its relativity; with *bhakti*, humility is self-abasement before the beauty of the Beloved everywhere present, self-annihilation before the Divine glory; with *karma*, the same virtue becomes the disinterested service of one's neighbor, the humiliation of self for the sake of God; but from a strictly yogic point of view, this same virtue will be in a way "geometrical" or "physical"; it will appear as a leveling of the activities of the animic substance, abstention from all mental affirmation.

The fact that the possibility of a spiritual technique results, not from a human willing, but from the nature of things, replies in advance to the objection — an all too human one — that Yoga is something useless, or even "artificial,"[2] and contrary to the true love of God. In reality, the yogic principle has its foundation in the cosmological aspect of man, an aspect that implies the possibility of applying to the microcosm disciplines which are "quasi-geometrical" and consequently as foreign to the circuitous ways of reasoning as to the impulses of sentiment; that is to say, these disciplines have a character that is purely "physical," using this term according to its primitive sense as applying to the whole realm of "concordant actions and reactions," hence to all that is subject to the impersonal laws and forces of the cosmos. On the other hand, when viewed according to a more profound perspective, the yogic principle is based on the idea that man is as though steeped in the Infinite: his essence — that by which he exists and knows — is "not other than" infinite just as a piece of ice is not other than the water in which it floats; man is "Infinity

---

2. It is too easily forgotten that according to such standards all sacraments and other rites would be "artificial," since their validity does not depend upon the mental or moral effort of the officiant.

congealed" — if one can express oneself thus. It is our hardness alone, the opacity of our fallen condition, that renders us impermeable to the pre-existing Grace; the practice of Yoga is the art of opening — on the basis of our cosmic structure — our carapace to the Light which infinitely surrounds us.[3] It will doubtless be objected that no technique could suffice in itself, that physical means could never alone and unaided permit man to transcend his own limits, that man is not simply a bundle of impersonal factors but also an intelligence and a will, therefore a living ego; this is evident, but it is precisely for this reason that yogic disciplines are always accompanied with intellectual and moral elements, elements of contemplation and virtue. Yoga does not "produce" sanctity; when reduced to its characteristic principle, it appears rather as a negative activity, comparable, say the Hindus, to the breaching of a dike: this operation, without producing anything by itself, permits water to flood a field. Only intellection — or love — can realize union positively, with God's help, and to the degree that belongs to them respectively.

The technical or impersonal character of yogic science links it to gnosis rather than to love, somewhat as the subjective character of musical emotion links it to the path of love rather than to that of gnosis.[4]

---

3. But which is, practically speaking and doubtless, "within us." "The Kingdom of God is within you," said Christ. And if he enjoins praying that "Thy Kingdom come," what is meant is not only universal regeneration, but also — and for all the more reason — the coming of the "Kingdom of Heaven" in our heart, which is like the point of intersection — or "strait gate" — towards the Infinite.

4. Christian mysticism comprises diverse modalities in time and space: there is in early Christianity, as in Islam, a distinction between "love" and "gnosis," but this distinction is not as systematic as in Hinduism. Christian *bhakti* stands apart from all gnosis and rests on the dogmas alone, while Christian *jñāna*, the gnosis of the Fathers the last echoes of which are to found among the Rhenish mystics, always includes — as with the Sufis — an element of love.

*

*   *

Semitic and European minds have a tendency towards irreducible alternatives, whereas the Hindu mind works readily by integrations and syntheses. It is difficult for a Westerner to reconcile the idea of a spiritual technique with an attitude of piety and virtue; this mixing of "coldness" and "warmth" seems to him to lack cohesion, sincerity and beauty; positions which are complementary seem to him to stand in irreducible opposition, whereas a Hindu without difficulty reconciles the apparent antagonisms, which he regards as poles of one and the same fundamental intention; he even goes so far as to consider his own fervor in an entirely objective manner, changing perspective in accordance with what is spiritually opportune. The European sees himself, practically speaking, before the following alternative: either he believes in piety, virtue, duty, moral beauty and the free gift of grace, in which case he will be prone to scorn the technical point of view and see in it nothing but "fakirism"; or else, reacting against religious sentimentalism, he opts for the yogic point of view (whether rightly or wrongly is not in question here), in which case he will tend to despise, or at least to undervalue piety and virtue and to uphold the "amoral" side of Yoga[5]; such a reaction, it must be said, is often sentimental in its own way, but in a "frigid" manner, and in that case we would without hesitation prefer pious sentimentality, which at least is what it purports to be. Be that as it may, the idea that the intellective assimilation of a symbol can replace or even

---

5. This impersonal and amoral — not "immoral" — character attaching to any strictly technical point of view does not prevent Yoga from being accompanied in fact by moral rules, nor does it preclude it from allying itself sometimes with sentimental attitudes as the case of *bhakti* proves; but it is not these associations that have tended to attract Westerners to the practices of Yoga.

surpass pious works shocks the individualism of those who affect not to believe in "techniques," and who — through lack of imagination on this plane — are far from surmising all that the practice of such apparently "easy" means entails morally.

Christianity is in its general structure a path of love; therefore the yogic element, which by its "objectivity" is related to gnosis, does not appear in the foreground; one encounters it in the Hesychast tradition — which includes aspects of gnosis from the very fact of its strict dependence on the Greek Fathers — but also, under a more sentimental form, in the mysticism of Saint John of the Cross. Doubtless it could be pointed out here — apart from any question of gnosis — that the love of God is not by definition sentimental, that it is above all the act of will that "chooses God," and that willing is not synonymous with emotivity: this is true when will depends on Knowing, but when such is not the case then will inevitably allies itself with feeling; because a path of pure willing is inconceivable, will depending always upon some factor that is either cognitive or emotive.

But, it will be argued, is not Hindu *bhakti* also a more or less emotive spirituality — and therefore after all passional? Our answer is that one must take into account the spiritual temperament of the Hindus, their contemplative plasticity, the particular character of their emotivity, which is more "cosmic" and less individualistic than that of Europeans, as well as more "aesthetic" and less prone to moralizing. Furthermore, the Hindu, while being a powerful logician, is little given to rationalism, a fact that must not be regarded as paradoxical, because he is above all an intuitive type whose intelligence is open to the essences of things; he does not live, like the Westerner, upon rational alternatives; metaphysical ideas, far from forming for him a more or less inoperative background, on the contrary intervene actively in his methods, even though their influence is doubtless less direct with the *bhakta* than with the *jnānī*.[6]

Aesthetic factors (giving this expression its most profound meaning) hold nearly the same importance in Hindu *bhakti* as intellectual factors; the same can be said of the *maḥabbah* of Sufism, as represented by Omar Ibn Al-Faridh, for example, or Jalal ad-Din Rumi. A European of Latin formation tends primarily to see in beauty as such passional attraction, seduction, or "the world"; in general he lacks the intuition of essences, the spontaneous sense for universal analogies and cosmic rhythms; he is given to replacing contemplative aestheticism by an ascetical form of sentimentality; he does not fall into ecstasy, like Ramakrishna, before some beauty of nature, or rather, before the celestial beauty therein reflected; it is rare for him to look on nature with the eyes of Saint Francis of Assisi. Music for a Westerner is indeed a sensible consolation, but it rarely amounts to more than that; he does not readily hear in it "the sound of the gates of Paradise opening and closing," according to an expression of the Mevlevi Dervishes;[7] he does not know sacred dance, although Saint Teresa of Avila had a presentiment of it and would certainly have appreciated its value.

6. It goes without saying that it is the traditionally minded Hindu we have in view, and not one whose hereditary dispositions have deviated in an anti-traditional direction, to the point of proving that *"corruptio optimi pessima."* Hinduism, strictly speaking, has no "dogmas" in the sense that every concept may be denied, on condition that the argument used is intrinsically true; which amounts to saying that concepts can be denied from the standpoint of a higher level of truth, metaphysics standing above cosmology and realization above theory as such. However, on their own level, the scriptural symbols of Hinduism are just as immovable as the Semitic dogmas, and this excludes any fallacious comparison of Hindu doctrine with the opinions of philosophers. No orthodox Hindu can maintain that the *Veda* has been mistaken on any point whatsoever.

7. "We have heard these sounds in Paradise," says Jalal ad-Din Rumi, "and although earth and water have thrown over us their veil, we retain dim memories of these celestial chants. . . . Music is the nourishment of those who love, for it recalls to them their primordial union with God."

The Westerner distinguishes above all between worldly or immoral beauty and beauty with a religious content — but on the other hand, since natural beauty binds him to passion instead of raising him towards the Infinite, he comes to identify passion with the beautiful, whence the loss of sacred art.[8] It is easy to understand why the *samkīrtanas* of the Hindu *bhaktas* or the "spiritual concerts" of the Sufis often appear to the Christian as a facile playing with emotion, and in point of fact a fluctuation between the intuition of the heart and natural emotion does exist, so much so that certain Sufis were opposed to the extension of these practices. Howbeit, the spiritual efficacy of aesthetic supports is in the nature of things; therefore it must actualize itself under certain conditions and it is unreasonable to deny this because of some moralizing preconception. From the yogic point of view everything capable of promoting concentration is by that fact utilizable, at least in principle; here the criterion of efficacy — apart from the intrinsic value of beauty — is therefore to be found in the unifying power of the aesthetic experience.

In order to clarify still further the difference between the Hindu and European mentalities, we can say this: the Christian, like every Monotheist — save in gnosis — finds himself situated intellectually between dogma and reason, whence the "obscurity of faith"; he is, as it were, suspended between divine mystery and human incapacity; intellection — supra-rational intuition — is then replaced by grace or "consolation." Such consolation is to be met with in all spirituality, Eastern as well as Western, for the simple reason

8. In the Middle Ages, the Eastern genius of Byzantium and the Nordic genius of the Celts and Germans contributed together to the flowering of Christian art; in the Renaissance the passional aspect of the artistic impulse killed the spiritual aspect of art; but as passional art wished in its turn to become religious, it sank fatally into a pompous hypocrisy and an empty aesthetical formalism. For the men of the Renaissance, beauty was made up of sensuality and rationalism; the latter dominated architecture and the former, plastic arts.

that it answers to a general possibility of the human soul; what is particular to Catholic mysticism is not the existence therein of consolations but their importance and the absence of analogous factors of another order and of an active nature. This restriction is not unrelated to a certain concern for collective expediency, for formal cohesion and apologetic convenience, or, in other words, to a tendency to reduce the mystical life to a single easily controllable type.

The problem of faith and consolation brings us to that of "temptations against faith": these are possible because faith is situated in the will and not in the intellect. Faith is a matter of grace, of will and of reason, at least in the perspective of love whereby Christian spirituality is determined in a quasi-exclusive manner; it has an aspect of "obscurity" which calls forth temptations, rather as the fallibility of reason calls forth errors, or as liberty in regard to evil calls forth sins. However, even when one takes faith in its ancient and integral sense, as including also, or even especially, gnosis, temptations nonetheless remain possible, but then they alter their characteristics: the rift between dogma and our strength of intuitive adherence to it is then replaced by the rift between intellectual certitude and human weakness, or rather it is the acute actualization of this rift that constitutes the trial. Christ's cry, *"Eli,Eli, lama sabachthani"* is the prefiguration of the mystical temptations against faith: just as the Christ is overwhelmed for an instant by the human obscurity He wills to taste in order that it may be vanquishable by man, so is the love of the mystic invaded by the obscurities of his own soul which the devils moreover have every interest in exploiting.[9] Contrary to what takes place with Christ, who embraces the entire cosmos, the mystic suffers only on his own account, unless he also, out of charity, expiates an obscurity foreign to

9. The Sufis regard doubt concerning the truth of the divine Unity as one of the temptations that can affect beginners in their retreats.

himself; such a human expiation will, moreover, necessarily remain partial.

A mysticism that is passional, and fraught with suffering by reason of this very feature, will readily see in the yogic technique a pretentious and facile attempt at shortcuts and avoidance of suffering;[10] from the standpoint of the Yoga-principle, as from the standpoint of pure gnosis, it is precisely the passional character of the mysticism of love which can take on an appearance of facility, though not in a blameworthy sense; "difficulty" will then reside not in suffering, but on the contrary in detachment and in a serenity which turns away from the passional and therefore "easy" movements of the soul; the difficulty in gnosis is subtle and qualitative, not dramatic. There is nothing individualistic about pure Yoga; it treats the plastic matter of the soul with a logic that is wholly impersonal, at least in principle and a priori.

In passional mysticism the negative character of ascetic voluntarism is compensated by sentimentality which, insofar as it is a human fact, is positive for man in the sense that it is not opposed to his nature, indeed quite the contrary; on the other hand, the passional and non-intellectual character of this voluntarism is compensated by the ascetic tendency of the sentimentality. As for intellective asceticism, it is neutral and serene; not penitential, but purificatory; it does not derive from regret for a sin; it is content to correct an error, since it is able to do so and to the extent that it is so able.

Gnosis requires impassivity based on truth, on the Immutable, not a suffering offered for the sake of love; we say it

10. This reproach of "facility" has often been formulated — and with what facility! — on the subject of the "Jesus Prayer," as if Christ had never said, "My yoke is easy and my burden is light. " There is not only the facility of means, there is also their holiness: the facility lies, for example, in the act of articulating a prayer, and their holiness in the divine character of the revelation that furnishes us with the prayer. Facility is a reproach only outside our receptiveness with regard to this sanctity.

does not "require," not that it cannot "admit" suffering, since by definition it admits all that is true on whatever grounds. For gnosis the emotive factor is not a usable key, except on the aesthetic plane where, however, this factor is compensated by the intellective aspect of beauty; one almost feels tempted to say that the *jnānī* is forever condemned to serenity. His point of departure could not be a passion for God; his nature is impregnated with contemplation and truth; it is fundamentally static; he follows his own immediate essence though he must necessarily integrate in his spiritual path all the tendencies belonging to human nature. This aspect of serenity, of profound peace, of "holy silence," is like the boundary stone marking the threshold of gnosis, but at the same time it is the essence thereof, the air gnosis breathes and lives by. We are here referring to gnosis as such, though without losing sight of the fact that it can enter into combinations with other paths and that differences here are in fact never absolute.

*
* *

We have tried to examine the reasons for the incompatibility that the majority of Europeans believe to exist between "virtue" — which attracts grace but does not create it — and "technique" which in their opinion seems to wish to appropriate grace artificially and in a spirit of presumptuous facility. No doubt the best way to show the perfect compatibility between these two principles is to define each of them as concretely as possible.

Virtue consists essentially in humility and charity; these are the fundamental qualities from which all others derive, to which they all relate and without which no sanctity is possible.[11] Humility presents itself under two aspects:

11. If the fundamental virtues are everywhere the same by reason of the unity of human nature, terminologies can vary greatly, because of a shift of emphasis according to differing mentalities. Thus, the Moslems

awareness of one's metaphysical nothingness in the face of the Absolute and awareness of one's personal imperfection; this second humility implies not only a relentless instinct for detecting one's own limitations and weaknesses, but also a simultaneous capacity to discern the positive qualities in one's neighbor, for a virtue which is blind to virtue in others destroys itself thereby.[12] Consciousness of one's individual insufficiency springs from the necessarily fragmentary character of the ego; in other words, to say "ego" is to say partial imperfection in regard to other individuals. Humility is moreover owed to all creatures, since all of them manifest qualities and glorify God after their manner; the first relation goes from God to the thing, and the second from the thing to God; man has a right to the things of creation only on condition that he respect them, that is to say on condition that he discern in each one both its divine property and its spiritual language; man never has a right to destroy simply for the pleasure of destroying. Among virtues the position of humility is a special one — like that of the apex in a triangle — because it conforms to God, not by "participation" but by "opposition," in the sense that the attitude of humility, poverty or self-effacement, is analogically opposed to the divine Majesty; this opposition is

prefer to lay stress on "poverty" *(faqr)* rather than on humility *(khushu, tadarra* or *towadu* according to the shade of meaning intended), humility being considered to be a mode of poverty. In place of charity they will rather speak of generosity *(karam)* and nobility *(sharaf)*, but they also tend to give much more importance to sincerity *(ikhlās)* and truthfulness *(ṣidq)* because these both imply the charitable virtues, whereas the contrary does not hold good in equal degree. The Moslem outlook stresses the aesthetic side of the virtues, rather than their sacrificial side as does the Christian outlook. Let us add that in Islam the origin of all sin is attributed not only to pride (of Satan refusing to do obeisance to Adam) but also to envy (of Cain killing Abel), both of these attitudes being contrary to "poverty" by reason of their pretension.

12. Pascal thought that the worst baseness is to claim glory for oneself, which is inaccurate and unjust; the worst baseness is to discredit the glory of others and to glorify one's own disgrace.

however a relative one, since it rejoins the direct analogy through its intrinsic perfection which is, *mutatis mutandis,* the simplicity of the Essence. Humility, therefore, is distinguishable from the other virtues by the fact that it marks a relatively indirect participation in the divine Prototype, or in other words by the fact that it is, depending on the point of view, either "more" or "less" than the other fundamental virtues.

As for charity, it consists in abolishing the egocentric distinction between "me" and the "other": it is seeing the "I" in the "other" and the "other" in the "I." Humility and charity are the two dimensions of self-effacement: they are, to use a Christian symbolism, like the vertical and horizontal branches of the Cross. The one can always be reduced to the other: humility is always to be found in charity, and conversely. To these two virtues must be added the virtue of veracity: it is love of truth, objectivity, impartiality; it is a virtue that situates intelligence in the framework of the will[13] — to the extent that the nature of things allows of this or demands it — and its function consists in keeping away every passional element from the intelligence. Discernment must remain independent of love or hate: it must see things as they are, firstly according to universal Truth which assigns to each thing its degree in the hierarchy of values, and secondly according to the truth proper to things in their immediate nature; when the alternative presents itself, preference must be given to essential aspects, for which accidental aspects must not be substituted, and so forth. This serenity

---

13. This feature veracity shares with faith, with the difference, however, that truth is "supernatural" in faith, whereas it can present any kind of nature in veracity. In common language, veracity sometimes becomes the fact of always speaking the truth but this definition is insufficient on the spiritual plane, firstly because every morality allows or even requires — according to the case — lying in case of necessity or "pious lying," and secondly because mere frankness does not in itself imply any objectivity of judgment, and lastly because virtue does not necessarily exclude error.

and this precision exclude neither love nor holy indignation, because these arise parallel to intellection and not within it: holy indignation, far from being opposed to truth, derives from truth as from its enabling cause. Truthfulness corrects any arbitrariness that might result from a humility or charity regarded in too subjective a way: it prevents humility from becoming an end in itself and thus sinning against intelligence and the nature of things; it likewise controls charity and determines its various modes. One has to be humble because the ego tends to think itself more than it is; and one has to be truthful because the ego tends to prefer its own tastes and habits to the truth.

Even at a purely intellectual level humility and charity are in fact far from being superfluous,[14] since the support of intellection is the human individual, who is not himself pure light; a contemplative mind, be it even one of prodigious acuteness, if it neglects these inward and essential virtues — perhaps out of simple forgetfulness — is not sheltered from error, at least on the plane of certain relativities, but not on the plane of principles nor in the setting of such infallibility as is safeguarded by conditions deriving from tradition. Certainly, the intellect implies and guarantees the fundamental virtues in proportion to its own "actualness," for which reason it is contradictory to attribute to a high metaphysical intelligence pride or egotism in the full and crude sense of those words; but there is almost always, between intellect and the man, a sufficient margin to justify a conscious effort towards moral perfection, for truth, like all noble things,

14. In the Christian perspective, veracity is found included in humility, which excludes prejudice, and in charity which excludes falsehood; in the Islamic perspective it is on the contrary veracity or sincerity that includes the other two virtues. These examples show that veracity is not of the same order as the more specifically volitional virtues.

has its own requirements. Man can do nothing without God; now virtue is to do nothing without God.[15]

When the virtues are not determined by a knowledge, an awareness of the nature of things, or, to be more exact, by an intuition of the divine qualities from which those things derive,[16] the virtues (with the exception of truthfulness) will inescapably be nourished on sentimentality, a fact that too often gives rise to a distressing confusion between virtue and feeling; and neither must one confuse a virtuous sentiment with a sentimental virtue.

Virtues in their own way manifest the truth; we have to know with all our being and not with intelligence alone; spiritual sincerity — or knowledge in its wholeness — demands something from us which, apart from all question of doctrinal or ritual form, comes entirely from ourselves, at least as regards the effort; for virtue in itself, in its ultimate content, can only come from Heaven. To be virtuous is to be perfectly oneself, it is to return to our primordial harmony, our ontological reality; without virtue all is either dispersed or else petrified, all becomes sterile. Virtue is the presence of the divine Being in the will and in sentiment just as beauty is the presence of the Divine in form. The soul belongs to the formal order: therefore it cannot participate in truth without beauty, it can only know

15. Saint Therese of Lisieux saw this clearly in her own manner: ". . . it would mean relying on my own strength, and when one is there, one risks slipping into the abyss. . . . I well understand how Saint Peter fell . . . he leaned on himself instead of leaning on the good God" (Counsels and Memories).

16. God is not "humble" like man, because He could not abase Himself before someone external and superior to Himself, for such a one does not exist. The "humility" of God, as we have said, is the simplicity of His essence, for He is without parts. There is, however, another aspect of the "divine humility," one that is both intrinsic and anthropomorphic: "When the servant takes one step towards his Lord the Lord gets up from his throne and takes one hundred steps to meet his servant" (*Ḥadīth* of the Prophet). As for man, he is not a pure essence, but a mixture of spirit and earth; therefore he cannot in himself be "good."

completely with the assistance of its own proper beauty, namely the virtue that ignores itself, that does not attribute itself to "me."[17] In other words, the direct and positive manifestation of Truth requires a framework that corresponds to it qualitatively: intellectual reality in practice has need of that "lived truth" that is virtue, which essentially is manifested as harmony of "proportions" and "rhythms"; in the microcosm as in the macrocosm, the Christic mystery implies the Marian mystery. Water reflects the moon only when it is calm, and this calm, this absorption of all discontinuous crispations into balance, is nothing other than beauty or virtue.

To transcend the virtues means, not to reject them in their positive contents, but to rejoin them in their universal and impersonal source, beyond the ego and in pure "being."

*
* *

Having described the element "virtue" in its broad lines, we must now attempt to define the element that is in a sense complementary to it, namely spiritual "technique," in order to demonstrate the perfect compatibility of these two elements in the spiritual life, or rather their interdependence. Previously we have seen that spiritual technique is essentially the art of concentration; now if the mind could be continually fixed upon the Absolute, "like oil flowing from a pot" as a Hindu text puts it, it would by that very fact be in an uninterrupted state of sanctity, first in a doubtless passive — but nonetheless salvific — way and then also necessarily in an active way. The fallen soul is like an untamed animal, all its tendencies are "centrifugal"; if it is true that virtue indirectly favors concentration, the latter in its turn favors virtue, by reason of the analogy between the center and quality; that is qualitative which manifests the

---

17. But not a virtue of which one has no awareness.

center. One could also say that the yogic aspect of virtue is our effort by which existential vice is laid open to the divine Virtue, while the virtuous aspect of Yoga is purity of intention. Concentration needs to be learned like any other art, such as the handling of a musical instrument or a weapon; the soul, if it is to be transformed by the beauty that is virtue — a beauty inconceivable outside truth, of which it is an expression — has also everything to gain by becoming supple in its "physical" substance through transformation of its very existential foundation; it is not enough for a viol to be well played, its wood must also be of noble quality. The yogic art, like every legitimate thing, draws its justification from its spiritual possibility, and it is enough to understand the latter in order to admit the former.

Strictly speaking, pure concentration is less a fixing of the mind upon an idea or an object than the elimination of every distraction; the divine presence, or grace if one so prefers, or the intellect, according to the point of view, must be allowed to act without hindrance, like a leaven; but concentration as such could not draw these out of nothing. As we have already made apparent, the virtues concern the content of the soul and yogic practices the container.

*
* *

The question of grace is inseparable from what we have just been considering. In spirituality three aspects are distinguishable, namely: virtue, art and grace. In virtue and art, man is active; before grace, he is passive or at least receptive. From the standpoint of virtue or merit, grace is a free gift; from the standpoint of technique or art, grace is consequent on one's power of concentration — but only in a partial manner — in conformity with the law of causality; but even in this case grace still retains its "gratuitous" character, since it never has a positive human cause, its positive cause always coming from God. Herein lies the profound meaning of the free gift of grace, for it is evident that this gratuitous imparting never signifies that God could be arbitrary or that grace might sometimes lack a sufficient cause. The cause of grace can never be found on the side of man except in a quite negative and accidental manner, for man can do no more than remove obstacles veiling the pre-existing grace, the immutable cause of which is the Infinite.[18] That is why Yoga is always referred to *Īshvara*, God regarded as "Being"[19]; without the initial grace of *Īshvara*, Yoga itself would be inconceivable. In an analogous sense the Sufis teach that the initiate can do nothing without the initial grace of *Allāh (tawfīq*, help of God) and that the spiritual states (*ahwāl*, plural of *hāl*) cannot be productions of any human industriousness, though this does not mean that man cannot take measures

18. Metaphysically speaking, it is a question here of a "relative infinitude," since everything comes to us from Being — except the ineffable essence of gnosis — and Being is not the Infinite in the absolute sense; Being nevertheless is absolute in relation to the creature as such. To state that the divine Person is limited would be, from a human point of view, worse than ill-sounding.

19. If for the theology of the Christian Scholastics (but not for the Patristic and Eckhartian gnosis) God is identified with Being, this is because that theology always corresponds to a way of love, whereas the theology of St. Gregory Palamas, for instance, who teaches that God contains Being without being reducible to it, allows for the possibility of gnosis. The *bhaktic* paths of India likewise consider Being only, the personal Divinity, in conformity with their own finality, which is only surpassed in *jnāna*. Yoga in the strict sense refers to *Īshvara* or the "personal God," because it envisages Him in his relations with the human microcosm, which is in fact the field of activity of all "spiritual technique." According to a rather common error found in certain circles, people think they are dealing only with *bhakti* wherever they meet an emotional element and with *jnāna* where they find intellectual dissertations; in reality, the valid criteria are as follows: where there is "ontologism" and "dualism" in a fundamental sense, it is a question of *bhakti*, but where there is "superontologism" and "non-dualism" *jnāna* is to be found; thus Meister Eckhart goes beyond the *bhaktic* point of view because, for him, God is "Being above Being and superessential Negation" and because "there is in the soul something uncreate and uncreatable."

to eliminate anything which might act as an obstacle to grace; indeed, if the powers of the lower and passional soul (*nāfs*) are able to cause the disappearance of a state of light, the powers of the superior and spiritual soul (*rūḥ*) can in their turn cause the disappearance of the effects of the inferior powers, therefore of those things that oppose themselves to grace in itself infinite. Furthermore, the state of grace must be fixed in the soul through efforts at once intellectual, moral and technical, or rather it is the soul that must be fixed in the state of grace, such fixation being called by the Sufis a "station"; but there are also graces or states (*ahwāl*) which quite clearly are independent of effort and in which the aspect of gratuitousness is directly manifested. God possesses infinitely the perfections of liberty and necessity, and both these aspects must express themselves in grace: the first is more particularly related to love and the second to gnosis.

It is important never to lose sight of the fact that there is no Yoga that presumptuously relies solely on its own resources, and that the most characteristic form of Yoga, namely the ensemble of *Hatha-Yoga* and *Raja-Yoga*, rests humbly at the feet of *Īshvara* and puts itself in the hands of God. This is because no "art," as we have said, any more than virtue or intellection, is possible without the grace of God. Virtue calls forth gratuitous grace — or grace in its manifestation as free gift — while spiritual art calls forth necessary grace, or rather the necessary manifestation of a grace in itself gratuitous; but the converse is equally true, though in an indirect way; virtue can, as a component of art, provoke a grace that will then appear like a consequence; these are imponderables such as a systematic presentation can barely touch on. Lastly, account must be taken of this: love, whose subject is man — and to the extent its subject is man — is at first separated from grace, whereas gnosis, whose subject is essentially the divine Intellect, is by its very nature a vehicle of grace and is so to the extent that gnosis, delivered from the passional bonds of a hardened human heart, reveals itself both as "that which knows" and "that which is known."

According to an approximate yet in many ways instructive distinction one can say that, if the virtues are concerned in a certain manner with the content of knowledge or love, inasmuch as that content coincides analogically with the divine qualities, the yogic art, for its part, is concerned with the act of knowing or loving, and so with the modalities of union. Virtue realizes in the human subject a conformity with the divine Object; spiritual art eliminates — or conjointly with knowledge contributes to eliminating — the human objectification that veils the divine Subject.

...overs. Moreover, a particular spiritual perspective is not discoverable somewhere within the framework of a tradition that excludes it; thus "theism" reappears in a certain sense, notably in the form of Amidhism, within the framework of Buddhism despite its characteristic non-theism; and this non-theism is to be found in its turn in the conception of the "impersonal Essence" of the Divinity in the monotheistic esoterisms; from the above examples it will be seen that religious frameworks have

Orthodoxy and Originality of Buddhism

The first question to be asked concerning any doctrine or tradition is that of its intrinsic orthodoxy; that is to say one must know whether that tradition is consonant, not necessarily with another given traditionally orthodox perspective, but simply with Truth. As far as Buddhism is concerned, we will not ask therefore whether it agrees with the letter of the Veda or if its "non-theism" — and not "atheism"! — is reconcilable in its expression with Semitic theism or any other, but only whether Buddhism is true in itself; which means, if the answer is affirmative, that it will agree with the Vedic spirit and that its non-theism will express the Truth, or a sufficient and efficacious aspect of the Truth, whereof theism provides another possible expression, opportune in the world it governs. Moreover, a particular spiritual perspective is usually discoverable somewhere within the framework of a tradition that excludes it; thus "theism" reappears in a certain sense, notably in the form of Amidism, within the framework of Buddhism despite its characteristic non-theism; and this non-theism is to be found in its turn in the conception of the "impersonal Essence" of the Divinity in the monotheistic esoterisms: from the above examples it will be seen that religious frameworks have nothing exclusive about them, and that it is always a question of emphasis or spiritual economy.[1]

What has just been said means implicitly that Buddhism, inasmuch as it is a characteristic perspective and independently of its modes, answers to a necessity: it could not but come to be, given that a non-anthropomorphic, impersonal and "static" consideration of the Infinite is in itself a possibility; such a perspective had therefore to be manifested at a cyclic moment and in human surroundings that rendered it opportune, for wherever the receptacle is, there the content imposes itself. It has sometimes been remarked that the Buddhist perspective is not distinguishable in any essential way from given doctrines or paths found in Hinduism; this is true in a certain sense — and is all the more likely inasmuch as Hinduism is characterized by an uncommon wealth of doctrines and methods — but it would be wrong to conclude from this that Buddhism does not represent as spontaneous and autonomous a reality as do the other great Revelations; what has to be said is that Buddhism is a "Hinduism universalized," just as Christianity and Islam — each in its own way — are a Judaism rendered universal, hence detached from its particular ethnic environment and made accessible to men of all manner of racial origins. It could be said that Buddhism extracted from Hinduism its yogic sap, not through a borrowing of course, but through a divinely inspired remanifestation; it imparted to this substance an expression that was simplified in certain respects,

---

1. The not infrequent employment, by the Buddha, of terms proper to Brahmanical theism clearly shows that the Buddhist perspective has nothing in common with atheism properly so called. "Extinction" or the "Void" is "God" subjectified; "God" is the objective "Void." If Buddhists — except in their perspectives of Mercy — do not objectify the Void or the Self, this is because they have nothing to ask of it, given their own anti-individualist point of view; if nevertheless there are certain "dimensions" where things appear otherwise, this is because the "objective aspect" of Reality is too much in the nature of things to pass unperceived and without being turned to account on occasion.

but at the same time fresh and powerfully original. This is demonstrated in a dazzling way by Buddhist art, the prototypes of which are doubtless found in the sacred art of India and in the yogic postures, or again in sacred dance which, for its part, is like an intermediary between yoga and temple statuary; Buddhist art — and here one is thinking chiefly of images of the Buddha — seems to have extracted from Hindu art, not such and such a particular symbolism, but its contemplative essence. The plastic arts of India evolve in the last analysis around the human body in its postures of recollection; in Buddhism the image of this body and this visage has become a symbol of extraordinary fecundity and a means of grace of unsurpassable power and nobility;[2] and it is this artistic crystallization that most visibly exteriorizes what Buddhism comprises of absoluteness and therefore also of universality. The sacred image transmits a message of serenity: the Buddhist Dharma is not a passionate struggle against passion, it dissolves passion from within, through contemplation. The lotus, supporting the Buddha, is the nature of things, the calm and pure fatality of existence, of its illusion, its disappearance; but it is also the luminous center of *Māyā* whence arises *Nirvāna* become man.

2. The genius of the yellow race has added to the Hindu prototypes something of a new dimension; new, not from the point of view of symbolism as such, but from that of expression. The image of the Buddha, after going through the Hellenistic aberration of Gandhara — providentially no doubt, for it is a question of the transmission of some secondary formal elements — reached an unheard of expansion among the yellow peoples: it is as if the "soul" of the Divinity, the nirvanic Beatitude, had entered into the symbol. The *Chitralakshana*, an Indo-Tibetan canon of pictorial art, attributes the origin of painting to the Buddha himself; tradition also speaks of a sandalwood statue which King Prasenajit of Shravasti (or Udayana of Kaushambi) had made during the very lifetime of the Buddha, and of which the Greek statues of Gandhara may have been stylized copies.

From the doctrinal point of view the great originality of Buddhism is to consider the Divine, not in relation to its cosmic manifestations as ontological Cause and anthropomorphic personification, but on the contrary in relation to its acosmic and anonymous character, hence as supra-existential "state," which will then appear as Voidness *(shūnyatā)* from the point of view of the false plenitude of existence *(samsāra)*; the latter is the realm of "thirst" *(trishnā)*. This perspective stresses the unconditional character of the divine Goodness, or rather of the nirvanic Grace which projects itself through a myriad of Buddhas and Bodhisattvas into the round of transmigration, even down to the hells; faith in the infinite Mercy of the Buddha — himself an illusory appearance of the beatific Void — already constitutes a grace or a gift. Salvation consists in leaving the infernal circle of "concordant actions and reactions"; and in this connection, morality appears as a quite provisional and fragmentary thing, and even as inoperative in the sight of the Absolute, since it is still involved in the indefinite chain of acts and the existential fruit of acts. Forms such as Zen and Amidism are particularly suited for allowing one to sense the subtle relationships, made of imponderables and paradoxes, which separate or connect the world of transmigration and Extinction, of *samsāra* and *Nirvāna.*

*

* *

In order to understand Buddhism in all its vast and varied extension, it is necessary to distinguish, in the Buddha himself, between his doctrine and his being: his doctrine, which is that of suffering, of the way of salvation and *Nirvāna;* his being, which first is manifested in the visible form of the Buddha — subsequently crystallized in sacred images — and then in the sermons of the latter part of his life, those on which the Mahayana is founded.

What we have called "the Buddha's being" refers to the merciful[3] and at the same time esoteric contents of his Message; this feature is even discernible in Theravadic Buddhism — despite the fact that it remains closed to the Mahayanic sutras — if only in the sacred image of the Buddha, the cult of which is prevalent in all countries of the Far East.

From a purely logical point of view, it might be objected that there is a contradiction between the basic teaching, which rejects any cult of the person of the Blessed One — the Law alone being regarded as the agent of salvation — and all the other elements which, on the contrary, crystallize around that person, his body and his name — whose spiritual heritage is dominant in Northern Buddhism; but both points of view are equally legitimate for, if it is true that logically the Message takes precedence over the Messenger, it is also true that the latter can be identified with the former and that the very instrument of the Revelation possesses the saving virtue of the Message; a certain relative opposition between two complementary dimensions of one and the same truth is in the nature of things. Here one has to recall the following saying of Christ: "It is expedient for you that I go away," and the fact that neither the Eucharistic Sacrifice nor the descent of the Holy Spirit would be conceivable without the departure of Jesus. We wish to say that the Buddha while still living on earth may reject all personalism, but that the Buddha once "departed" must be all the

---

3. The *Gītā-Govinda* of Jayadeva, an orthodox Hindu text, says of the Buddha: "Through pity (for living beings), thou hast not observed the Vedic prescriptions for (blood) sacrifice, when thou sawest how the animals were killed; Keshava (Vishnu), Thou within the body of the Buddha, Thou art victorious, Hari (Vishnu), Lord of the universe!" Seen from this standpoint, the Buddha's message makes one think of the abolition of human sacrifice by Abraham; but the basis of the idea here is that Buddhism comprises a message of mercy or "non-violence" *(ahimsa)* and that it is in this aspect that Hinduism can "situate" it.

more "present"; the Law and the Person, the Message and the Messenger henceforth are one.

To understand the teaching of the Buddha the following must be borne in mind: namely that it is founded a priori on the concrete fact of human experience in general under its most immediate and tangible aspect, with provisional omission of every element that does not enter directly into that experience. Now the Buddha, as spokesman of this perspective, could not exteriorize his own saving nature on the very plane of a Law which, by the logic of things, confers the whole initiative of Deliverance on man himself.[4] This saving nature is evident, since there must be a sufficient cause to account for the fact that it is he, Shakyamuni, and not some other man, who found the way out of the karmic wheel of births and deaths — or rather that particular way which is specifically Buddhic and which alone is in question here — and that it is he alone who "has broken his existence like a breastplate." This uniqueness of function or miracle, which at first effaces itself before the Law, not being its content, had to assert itself in its turn and in its own nature, in its quality of divine gift; which it did, firstly under the form of the monastic initiation[5] and secondly through the later sermons.[6] These sermons

---

4. In an analogous way, did Christ not say: "God alone is good," and did he not pray, like a simple mortal, despite his divinity? Did he not at first restrict his Message to just the people of Israel? For anyone who knows Christianity, there is no difficulty here — any more than in the fact that Christ was baptized when young. But a certain logical contradiction exists nonetheless, and a Buddhist could draw an argument from it, if he were interested in doing so, as a Christian could, conversely, make something of the "Buddhist contradiction" in order to deny the supernatural character of Buddhism. The fact that, contrary to what happened with the Buddha, Christ declared his divinity and even made it the pillar of his Message, only accentuates certain difficulties, at least from a very outward point of view.

5. This obviously presupposes an initiatory power and consequently a "divine nature."

6. It should not be forgotten that some of these Scriptures belong not only to the Mahayana, but also to Theravada Buddhism.

are noticeably different from those embodying the Law; they reveal the metaphysics of the Void, which will subsequently take on a doctrinal aspect with Nagarjuna and a purely "experimental" aspect with the school of *Dhyāna* or Zen, whose great initiator was Bodhidharma; the "Flower Sermon," a silent gesture, is evidently independent of any written formulation. Yet another expression of the "personal reality" of the Buddha is the saving invocation of the name of Amitabha and lastly, as we have said, the sacramental image of the *Tathagāta*, true "manifestation of the Void" (*shūnyamūrti*) and "expression of the inexpressible." All these elements derive from the aspect that we have called the "being" of the Buddha, by way of distinguishing it from his general and more or less "outward" doctrine.

*

* *

The "Great Vehicle" possesses a mysterious dimension known as the "Adamantine Vehicle" (Vajrayana); in order to grasp its meaning, one has to first understand what we repeatedly have termed the "metaphysical transparency of the world," that is to say one has to base oneself on a perspective according to which — to quote an expression of Pascal's we favor — Reality is "an infinite sphere whose center is everywhere and its circumference nowhere": it is this circumference and this center which are represented, in the adamantine doctrine, by the Buddha Mahavairochana (in Japanese Dainichi Nyorai)[7] who is at one and the same time — in Vedantic terms — *Ātmā, Īshvara* and *Buddhi*; that is to say Supra-ontological Essence, Ontological Essence and Universal Intellect. This metaphysical transparency everywhere refers the effect back to the Cause without, however, doing away with the irreversibility of the

7. The Japanese heir to this current is Shingon — founded by the illustrious Kobo Daishi, one of the fathers of Japanese civilization — and also Tendai, whose founder was Dengyo Daishi.

causal relationship; the Absolute is nowise causal in itself, since in reality nothing can be outside It, but It is causal from the point of view of the cosmos which is real only as effect and in virtue of the metaphysical reduction of the effect to the Cause. Thus "all is *Ātmā*," or all is *Shūnya* ("Void") or Vairochana — or "solarity" if we bear in mind the etymology as well as the symbolism of this Sanskrit name — but no thing is in itself, in its accidentality the "Self" or the "Void" or the "solar Buddha."

We may specify the structure of this metaphysical "vision" by having recourse to the following symbol: the spider's web, formed of warp and weft threads — or of radii and concentric circles — represents the Universe under the twofold relationship of essential identity and existential separation; the synthesis of these two relationships will be indicated by the spiral. From the point of view of the radii, a given thing "is" the Principle; from the point of view of the concentric circles, a given thing only "represents" It; from the point of view of the spiral, however, we shall say that a given thing is an "emanation" or "manifestation," therefore that it is neither the Principle as such nor simply an image of It. Grosso modo it can be said that the West — namely European philosophy and Semitic exoterism — is rather attached to the second relationship, that of concentric circles and of existential discontinuity or separation, whereas the East — namely Semitic esoterism and Asian metaphysics — will prefer the first relationship, that of radii and identity of essence, therefore of "metaphysical transparency." It is an error — inevitable[8] in exoterism — to believe that "creation" is an absolutely closed and quasi-autonomous system; that it is "absolutely creation" in the same way God is "absolutely God"; God is "absolutely Himself," but the world is only "relatively world" because, if there is on the one hand a "relatively absolute," there can

8. Which is to say that exoterism cannot avoid choosing a "lesser truth" in view of a "lesser evil."

never be on the other hand an "absolutely relative." It is true that creation as such is entirely created, but precisely these words "as such" neither cover all its nature nor explain its possibility. But to return to the spider and its symbolism: this, with the solar form of its web, evokes Being — or the Self — which draws forth the Cosmos from itself and "eats" the beings to be found within it; "deification" is to be assimilated by God.

The great truth — or the great experience — represented by the Vajrayana is to show that each thing, each energy, by the very fact that it exists — and that, existing, it is "something" of That which makes it exist — constitutes a possible entry towards Deliverance; universal Buddhahood implies that each consciousness, being essentially Buddha, can "become That which is." If one may define esoterism as a "shortcut" not within reach of every mental make-up or every degree of intellectual scope, the Adamantine Vehicle, with its perspective of "ubiquity" and its quasi-theurgic method of mantra, provides a particularly conclusive example of what constitutes an esoteric method.

In this connection it is worth recalling here a highly suggestive comparison once made to the author by a Japanese Buddhist: the sound of Christian bells, so he was saying, draws man upward and leads him away from the world; but the heavy and deep sound of the Buddhist bell leaves us motionless, it makes us come down into ourselves, into our supra-personal Center. Here is an instructive confrontation of two spiritual rhythms which, however, has nothing irreducible about it: on the one side there is "dynamic elevation," sublimation of "becoming," while on the other there is "static profundity," essence of being.

*

* *

The idea of "universal illusion" or the unreality of the world, of *Māyā*, constitutes something like an insurmountable barrier between Western "personalism" and Oriental metaphysics: Hindus are reproached for denying the world or on the contrary for identifying the world with God, and Buddhists are blamed for denying the soul — as if *Nirvāna* were not the prototype of the soul and its summit — and in so doing the would-be critics do not ask themselves what part is played in all this by terminological contingencies; for only too often it happens that discussion begins about attributes before there has been agreement about things in themselves. Buddhists deny "the soul," so it is said, and yet they essentially admit the "karmic" continuity or, if one prefers, the moral causality of that living and conscious nucleus that is the ego.

Individuation takes place to the degree that the movement of the cosmic wheel is rapid: just as water when agitated becomes dispersed in innumerable drops, so likewise the Self becomes segmented, so to speak — but in illusory mode and without thereby being affected in its immutability — into innumerable particular subjects: the current of forms becomes the torrent of souls. The current of forms is at once movement and division; where the rotation of the cosmic wheel takes place, there also occurs the dispersal of souls, individuation with its countless modalities; the ego is a quasi-"physical" consequence of this universal rotation. Where there is calm, there also is access to the immutable and indivisible Self; where the center is, there Unity is. And as the cosmic wheel is "none other" than the Self, on pain of non-existence, so also the Self can arise everywhere as a saving miracle.

The very absurdity of the plurality of egos proves that this can be but a question of an "optical illusion" on the macrocosmic scale, of an existential disequilibrium which, as such, cannot continue indefinitely; each ego is a flagrant contradiction, a "scandal" that reason comes up against just as it does against the "finite infinity" of time and space. The empirical "I" is nothing but a shifting tissue of images and tendencies; when the ego of an individual eight years old is compared with the ego of the same individual at eighty years of age one may well ask oneself where the real "I" is. And if a man could live for a thousand years, what would remain of that which was his "I" in the first century of his life? Beings and events would drift around him like leaves scattered by the wind, the sky itself would end by becoming a crushing burden, his body would be like a coffin — unless the man were to surmount his ego and thus perceive the Face of God in all things, like a new sky whose infinity stabilizes and liberates; but then this very world would no longer be "of this world" for that man; it would be a kind of hereafter. Man becomes attached to his scanty memories because he in practice confuses these with his own self, as if there were not to be found outside him, before and after him impressions, destinies, memories fairer or richer than his own and to which he will never have access; and as if a mental image, whatever its value, could forever be identified with one's immortal personality. Man is incapable of viewing an object from all sides at once or under all its aspects — it is impossible for him to enjoy at the same time every aspect of a precious thing or a beloved being; in the carnal ecstasy, the creature can no longer enjoy any visual perception of form, and this is an impoverishment even while foreshadowing the extinction of the soul in God. Bliss is possible only beyond all those formal crystallizations to which passion clings; that is why in earthly pleasure one thing precludes another, why all is measured out in space and time and why one happiness always implies the forgetfulness, if one may so put it, of a thousand other possible happinesses.

The foregoing considerations bring us closer to the Buddhist — and the Vedantic — idea of the unreality of the world;[9] in order to render this idea more familiar, a certain

---

9. Sufism, as is known, comprises the same doctrine, as is born witness to by this passage of the *Gulshan i Raz* of Mahmud Shabistari: "The world is an imaginary form, diffused shadow of the Infinite ... the imagination produces objective phenonmena having no real existence; in the same

imaginative power can be called into play by posing the question in an inverse sense: what then is the meaning of the common belief that the world is real, absolutely real? How can one call "real," without applying the slightest attenuation of meaning, phenomena which become practically reduced to nothing, not indeed in their immediate surroundings, but as soon as one considers space and time in all their extension? No one denies the relative reality of a given tree, a fleck of foam, a dream; but what does that tree represent on the scale of the galaxies and what does its brief life mean, even if it lasts for centuries, in relation to geological periods, reducible to mere instants in their turn? What is the reality of a tiny drop of water beside the ocean and its ages-long existence? People will no doubt reply that everyone knows in some sense that time is relative, but this is not the question, for there is knowledge and then there is knowledge: what man ever "lives" in a concrete sense both the simultaneity and the evanescence of things, to the point of being able to transcend himself and by that very fact to grasp the dreamlike character of the current of forms? But there is also ignorance on the plane of naturally simultaneous things, that is to say there is the inability of most men to "be" others, to live two lives or all lives at once, so to speak: if man feels so much at ease within his limits, this is because his imagination does not allow him to be conscious of what is happening to other people, on other continents, in other spiritual worlds. In fact, a lack of imagination is for many a condition of happiness since it helps to confer that easy assurance which most men need in order to feel happy, failing a happiness of a superior order gained on the ruins of a previous equilibrium; it might almost be

way, this world has no substantal reality, but is only a play of shadows or a game. All is penetrated by absolute Being, in its infinite perfection. There are many numbers, but only One alone counts. . . . The house has been left empty, except for the Truth, because the world disappeared in an instant."

said that man needs errors in order to be able to sleep peacefully.

The Divine Intellect, free of all infirmity, knows things both in their succession and in their simultaneity: it beholds the logical unfolding of things as well as their global possibility; knowing the substances, it knows at the same time the accidents, at the level of reality — or unreality — that is theirs. Some man in the Middle Ages is walking in some town and thinks he is living "at this present moment," in which supposition he is not more deceived than ourselves of course; now if that man while crossing his street thinks deeply of God, he will immediately shed the aspect of temporal and spatial illusion that separated him from us; the street, in its false "actuality," limits him no longer, he has come out of the deceptive instantaneity of his corporal, spatial and psychological situation; while thinking of God he is at our side, and not only that: he is everywhere, at the side of all men, in all worlds; he is in a sense wherever one has thought of the Absolute[10] and wherever It will be thought of; and thus maintaining himself in the center, he is like a witness of all things; any question of unconsciousness — or of "lack of imagination" — then no longer counts, for it is as if he were endowed with a consciousness of everything, from the moment that his mind is directed on the divine Void and that thereby he becomes situated at the center of space and time.

But there is not only the question of the unreality of the cosmos; there is also the question of its relative reality, therefore of the identity of essence — a mysterious and almost ineffable identity — between manifestation and the Principle or between symbols and their Prototype: in "such and such" a light or "such and such" an intelligence, we meet Light or Intelligence "as such," therefore all the light

10. This could refer to an Absolute still relative in itself; but this "relative Absolute" — creative and saving Being — is absolute in relation to man as such; it is relative only *in divinis* and in the Intellect.

and intelligence there is: the word "such" first expresses particularity or accidentality and after, in the expression "as such," it expresses essence or reality, the divine Suchness. That which is not identical is different; that which is not different is identical; the world — macrocosm or microcosm — is "neither divine nor non-divine," or it possesses both qualities at once. Formulations of this kind, apparently simplified to the point of unreason — as commonly happens with antinomian expressions — demand more than simple logic for their understanding, they call into play that which, in the intelligence, is most mysterious according to the saying: "He (God) put his eye into their hearts, that he might show them the greatness of his works" (Ecclesiastics 17:8).

*

*   *

In conclusion, we will quote a passage taken from the works of the great Japanese sage, Honen, in his *Summary of Nembutsu Doctrine*: "We find in the many teachings the great Master (the Buddha) himself promulgated during his lifetime, all the principles for which the eight Buddhist sects, the esoteric and exoteric and the Greater and the Lesser Vehicles (Mahayana and Hinayana) stand, as well as those elementary doctrines suited to the capacity of the immature, together with those intended for men capable of grasping Reality itself. Since then there have been various expositions and commentaries on them such as we now have, with their multitude of diverse interpretations. Some expound the principle of the utter emptiness of all things. Some bring us to the very heart of reality, while others set up the theory that there are five fundamental distinctions in the natures of sentient beings, and still others reason that the Buddha-nature is found in them all. Every one of these sects claims that it has reached the goal through its world view, and so they keep contending with one another, each persisting that its own perspective is the most profound and is absolutely right. Now the fact is that what they all say is exactly what the Sutras and Shastras say, and corresponds with the golden words of Nyorai (the Buddha) himself who, according to men's varying capacity, taught them at one time one thing and at another time another, as circumstances required . . . If we but attend to our religious practices as the Sutras teach, they will all help us to pass safely over the sea of births and deaths to the other shore . . ." The end of this passage evokes the famous formula of the two *Prajnā-Pāramitā-Hridaya-Sūtras*: "Gone, gone; gone for the other shore; attained the other shore; O Enlightenment, be blessed!" *(Gāte, gāte; pāragāte; pārasamgāte; Bodhi, svāhā!)*[11]

11. *Honen, the Buddhist Saint, His Life and Teaching.* Translation by Rev. Harper Havelock Coates and Ringaku Ishizuka; Kyoto, 1949.

3. His name (technology) term is "The Great Architect of the Universe", but He is also a painter, sculptor, musician and poet there is a Hindu symbolism which represents Him as creating and destroying the world as He dances.

Principles and Criteria of Art

Once again we would draw attention to the fundamental importance of art both in the life of a collectivity and in the contemplative life,[1] an importance arising from the fact that man is himself "made in the image of God"[2]: only man is such a direct image, in the sense that his form is an "axial" and "ascendant" perfection and his content a totality. Man by his theomorphism is at the same time a work of art and also an artist; a work of art because he is an "image," and an artist because this image is that of the Divine Artist.[3] Man alone among earthly beings can think, speak and produce works; only he can contemplate and realize the Infinite. Human art, like Divine Art, comprises both determinate and indeterminate aspects, aspects of necessity and of freedom, of rigor and of joy.

This cosmic polarity enables us to establish a primary distinction, namely the distinction between sacred and profane art: in sacred art what takes precedence over every-

---

1. See the chapter on "Forms in Art" in *The Transcendent Unity of Religions* (The Theosophical Publishing House, 1993) and that on "Aesthetics and Symbolism" in *Spiritual Perspectives and Human Facts* (Perennial Books, 1987).

2. In the words of the Bible (Translator's note).

3. In Masonic terminology God is "The Great Architect of the Universe," but He is also a painter, sculptor, musician and poet; there is a Hindu symbolism which represents Him as creating and destroying the worlds as He dances.

thing else is the content and use of the work; whereas in profane art these are but a pretext for the joys of creation. If within the framework of a traditional civilization art doubtless is never wholly profane, it may however become relatively so precisely because its motive force is to be found less in symbolism than in the creative instinct; such art is thus profane through the absence of a sacred subject or a spiritual symbolism but traditional through the formal discipline that governs its style. The position of non-traditional art is quite different: here there can be no question of sacred art and at most it may be called profane religious art; moreover the motive of such art is "passional" in the sense that an individualistic and undisciplined sentimentality is placed at the service of religious belief. Whether profane art is naturalistic and "religious," like Christian art of modern times, or both traditional and worldly, like medieval European or Indo-Persian miniatures or Japanese woodcuts, it often presupposes an extra-sacerdotal point of view and so a "worldliness" such as makes its appearance at a relatively late stage in the theocratic civilizations. In primordial periods art always was limited to either objects of ritual use or working tools and household objects, but even such tools and objects were, like the activities they implied, eminently symbolical and so connected with ritual and with the realm of the sacred.[4]

This brings us to a most important point: to a great extent sacred art ignores the aesthetic aim; its beauty arises above all from its spiritual truth and so from the exactitude of its

---

4. Highly significant is the reaction of a Sioux chief (quoted by Charles Eastman in *The Indian Today*) on being shown a picture gallery. "So this is the white man's strange wisdom," he exclaimed. "He cuts down the forests which have stood in pride and grandeur for centuries, he tears up the breast of our mother the earth and befouls the streams of clear water; without pity he disfigures the paintings and monuments of God and then bedaubs a surface with color and calls it a masterpiece!" In this connection it must be pointed out that the painting of the Red Indians is a writing, or, to be more precise, a pictography.

symbolism and from its usefulness for purposes of ritual and contemplation, and only secondarily from the imponderables of personal intuition; in fact this alternative could not present itself. In a world which knows no ugliness on the level of human products — a world, in other words, to which error in forms is still unknown — aesthetic quality cannot be a primary consideration; beauty is everywhere, beginning with nature and with man himself. If aesthetic intuition in the deepest sense has its own importance in certain modes of spirituality, only in a secondary manner does it enter into the genesis of a work of sacred art; in that process, beauty, first of all, does not have to be a direct aim, and then it is ensured by the completeness and integrity of the symbol and by the traditional quality of the work.[5] This must not, however, make one lose sight of the fact that a feeling for beauty, and so also a need for beauty, is natural in normal man and is indeed the very condition behind the detachment of the traditional artist in regard to the aesthetic quality of sacred work; in other words a major preoccupation with this quality would for him amount to a pleonasm. Not to feel the need for beauty is an infirmity, not unrelated to the inescapable ugliness of the machine age, which under industrialism has become widespread; since it is impossible to get away from industrialism people make a virtue of this infirmity and calumniate both beauty and the need for it: this is like the proverbial saying that he who wants to drown his dog, accuses it of rabies. Those whose interest lies in the public assassination of beauty seek to discredit it by the use of such terms as "picturesque" and

5. Professed aesthetes are inevitably profane in their point of view; they betray their insufficiency by the air of unintelligence apparent both in their art and in the way they exercise their choice, as well as by the fact that on certain levels their taste always tends to be somewhat coarse. For most Europeans of the 18th and 19th centuries icons were "ugly"; it may be that their own work is not exactly ugly, but it is certainly lacking in truth and intelligence in most cases.

"romantic" — just as people seek to suffocate religion by labeling it "fanaticism" — and by passing off what is ugly and trivial as "realistic"; this is to reduce beauty to a mere luxury of painters and poets. The cult of chance — of a chance that is ugly and trivial — betrays just the same intention: the "world as it is" is but ugliness and triviality garnered in the chaos of coincidences.[6] There is an affectation of angelic virtue which pretends to circumvent this problem by an appeal to "pure spirit" and is all the more unpleasant for being allied to the so-called "sincerity" of the man claiming to be "dedicated" or "authentic." When things are looked at in this way people soon come to regard as "spiritual" — because "sincere" — things which are the very antipodes of all spirituality. The abolition of beauty, whether sincere or not, means the end of the intelligibility of the world.

To return to the main question: if sacred art expresses what is spiritual either directly or indirectly, profane art must also express some value, unless it is to lose all legitimacy; the value it expresses, apart from the value of which every traditional style is the vehicle, is, first, the cosmic quality of its content and, secondly, the virtue and intelligence of the artist. Here it is therefore the subjective value of the man which predominates, but — and this is essential — that value is determined by the sacred, by the fact that the artist is integrated into a traditional civilization the genius of which he inevitably expresses; in other words he makes himself the exponent, not only of personal, but also

6. In France, for instance, advertisement posters are spread about like some filthy and insolent gangrene devouring the countryside; they are to be found not merely in towns but also in the tiniest hamlets and even on isolated ruins, and this is equivalent to the destruction, or partial destruction, of both country and fatherland. We write thus, not in the name of the picturesque, which does not interest us in the slightest, but in defense of the soul of a people. Such desperate triviality is like the trademark of the machine, which seeks to devour our souls, and is thus shown up as "the fruit of sin."

of collective values, since both alike are determined by the tradition in question. The genius is at the same time traditional and collective, spiritual and racial, and then personal; personal genius is nothing without the concurrence of a deeper and wider genius. Sacred art represents above all the spirit, and profane art the collective soul or genius, but this of course presupposes that it is integrated into the tradition. Taken together spiritual and collective genius make up traditional genius which gives its imprint to the whole civilization.[7]

*

*   *

Before going further we should perhaps define the "sacred," although it belongs to that category of things which are blindingly clear. But precisely because of this very clarity, such realities have become for many people incomprehensible, as is also true, for example, of "being" and "truth." What then is the sacred in relation to the world? It is the interference of the uncreate in the created, of the eternal in time, of the infinite in space, of the supraformal in forms; it is the mysterious introduction into one realm of existence of a presence which in reality contains and transcends that realm and could cause it to burst asunder in a sort of divine explosion. The sacred is the incommensurable, the transcendent, hidden within a fragile form belong-

7. In traditional art are to be found creations — or rather what might well be called revelations — which may appear unimportant to those who are prejudiced in favor of individual "masterpieces" as well as from the standpoint of the "classical" categories of art; but these creations are nonetheless among the irreplaceable works of human genius. Such are the Nordic decorations, so rich in primordial symbols, the motifs of which are also to be found in the folk art of most European countries and indeed even in the depths of the Sahara; such also are the Abyssinian processional crosses, the Shinto *toriis*, the majestic eagle-feather head-dresses of the American Indians and the Hindu *saris* in which splendid dignity is combined with grace.

ing to this world; it has its own precise rules, its terrible aspects and its merciful qualities; moreover any violation of the sacred, even in art, has incalculable repercussions. Intrinsically the sacred is inviolable, and so much so that any attempted violation recoils on the head of the violator.

The supernatural value of sacred art arises from the fact that it conveys and communicates an intelligence which is lacking in the collectivity. Like virgin nature it has a quality and function of intelligence which it manifests through beauty because in essence it belongs to the formal order; sacred art is the form of the Supra-formal, it is the image of the Uncreate, the language of Silence. But as soon as artistic initiative becomes detached from tradition, which links it to the sacred, this guarantee of intelligence fails and stupidity shows through everywhere: aestheticism is moreover the very last thing that can preserve us from this danger.

An art is sacred, not through the personal intention of the artist, but through its content, its symbolism and its style, that is, through objective elements. By its content: the subject represented must be as prescribed either when following a canonical model or in a wider sense; always, however, it must be canonically determined. By its symbolism: the sacred personage, or the anthropomorphic symbol, must be clothed or adorned in a given manner and not differently and may be making certain gestures but not others. By its style: the image must be expressed in a particular hieratic formal language and not in some foreign or imagined style. In brief, the image must be sacred in its content, symbolical in its detail and hieratic in its treatment; otherwise it will be lacking in spiritual truth, in liturgical quality and — for all the more reason — in sacramental character. On pain of losing all right to existence, art has no right to infringe these rules and has the less interest in doing so since these seeming restrictions confer on it, by their intellectual and aesthetic truth, qualities of depth and power such as the individual artist has very small chance of drawing out of himself.

The rights of art, or more exactly of the artist, lie in the technical, spiritual and intellectual qualities of the work; these three qualities are so many modes of originality. In other words the artist can be original through the aesthetic quality of his work, by the nobility or piety reflected in it and by the intelligence or knowledge which enables him to find inexhaustible variations within the framework laid down by tradition. All sacred art proves that this framework is relatively wide: it does indeed restrict incapacity but not either talent or intelligence. True genius can develop without making innovations: it attains perfection, depth and power of expression almost imperceptibly by means of the imponderables of truth and beauty ripened in that humility without which there can be no true greatness. From the point of view of sacred art or even from that of merely traditional art, to know whether a work is an original, or a copy is a matter of no concern: in a series of copies of a single canonical model one of them, which may be less "original" than some other, is a work of genius through a concatenation of precious conditions which have nothing to do with any affectation of originality or other posturing of the ego.

Apart from its function as a direct aid to spirituality, sacred art is indispensable as a support for the intelligence of the collectivity: to abolish sacred art as was done in the Renaissance or in Greece in the fifth century B.C. is to abolish that intelligence — one might say that intellectuality — and so to give free rein to a sensibility that is passional and henceforth ungovernable.[8] Moreover the theological function of religious art must not be overlooked: art should by its determinate aspects teach revealed truths, that is, by

8. It is, of course, the "collective intelligence" which is here in question, not intelligence in itself: Greek decadence did not affect the spirit of a man like Plato. If, however, the collective intelligence is compromised, that clearly will render the unfolding of particular intelligences more uncertain. What Greek decadence had destroyed, Christianity recreated to last for a thousand years.

its types or models, and it should suggest spiritual perfumes by subtle aspects which will depend on the intuition of the artist. Now, naturalistic religious art makes truth hard to believe and virtue odious for the simple reason that in it truth is overwhelmed by the stridency of a necessarily false description and virtue is drowned in an almost unavoidable hypocrisy; naturalism compels the artist to represent what he could not have seen as if he had seen it, and to manifest sublime virtue as if he himself possessed it.

This teaching function is also incumbent, though far less directly, on profane art when it is linked to the tradition by its style and by the mentality of the artist; in European medieval miniatures can be discerned an expression of the Christian spirit doubtless indirect, but nonetheless intelligible. The opportuneness of profane art is, however, psychological rather than spiritual, so that it always remains something of a two-edged sword or a "lesser ill" and one must not be surprised at the severe condemnations launched against profane art in periods still stamped with a sacerdotal outlook. Here as in other fields the functions of things may vary according to circumstances.

*
* *

Scriptures, anagogy and art are derived from Revelation though at very different degrees. Scriptures are the direct expression of the Speech of Heaven, whereas anagogy is its inspired and indispensable commentary[9]; art constitutes as it were the extreme limit or material shell of the tradition and thus, by virtue of the law that "extremes meet," rejoins what is most inward in it, so that art is itself inseparable from inspiration. Anagogy is the vehicle for metaphysical

9. We are referring to essential commentaries whose inspiration, though secondary, is nonetheless a necessary concomitant of Revelation; other commentaries, whether metaphysical, mystical or legal, may not be indispensable.

and mystical intelligence — aside from its purely legal interpretation — whereas art is the support of the collective intelligence and is contingent to the same degree as is the collectivity as such. In other words, scriptural Revelation is accompanied by two secondary currents, the one inward and indispensable for contemplative men, the other outward and indispensable for the generality of people. For the sage there is no common measure between the commentary on Scripture and art; he may even do without the latter provided it be replaced by a void or by virgin nature and not by a falsified art. For the tradition as a whole, however, art assumes an importance almost as great as exegesis, since tradition cannot manifest itself apart from forms. Again, if the elite have far more need of exegesis than of art, the generality of people have on the contrary far more need of art than of metaphysical and mystical doctrines; but, since the elite depend "physically" on the whole collectivity, they too indirectly have need of art.

Commentary in the widest sense, however, comprises an aspect that is outward because it treats, among other things, of exoteric questions. Conversely, art has an aspect that is inward and profound by virtue of its symbolism; it then fulfills a different function and speaks directly to the contemplative mind: in this way it becomes a support for intellection, thanks to its non-mental, concrete and direct language. Besides the metaphysical and mystical commentary on Scripture there is a legal and moral commentary addressed to the community as a whole, just as there is, besides the formal and collective function of art, a function that is strictly spiritual and esoteric. Seen from the latter point of view, art will be more inward and more profound than verbal expositions, and this explains the central function which a sacred image, such as that of the Buddha, can assume. There is a highly significant connection between the loss of a sacred art and the loss of anagogy, as is shown by the Renaissance: naturalism could not kill symbolism — sacred art — without humanism killing anagogy and, with it, gnosis. This is so because these two elements, anagogical science and symbolical art, are essentially related to pure intellectuality.[10]

*

* *

Of Hindu figurative art it can be said that it is derived from the postures and gestures of yoga and of the mythological dance. Dancing, the divine art of Shiva-Nataraja, the Lord of the Dance, was revealed to the sage Bharatamuni by Shiva and His spouse Parvati themselves and was codified by the sage in the *Bharata-Natya-Shāstra*. Hindu music, closely connected as it is with dancing, is founded on the *Sāma-Veda*, its rhythms being derived from the Sanskrit meters. It is dancing which provides the determining note of the whole of Hindu art: sacred images translate this figurative mythology — or figurative metaphysic — into the language of inert matter.[11] Let us add that this art is neither

10. Guénon wrote somewhere that the Middle Ages were the only period in which the West as a whole knew a true intellectual development; and it was not by chance that this was also the only period in which the West knew a sacred art, if in both cases we leave aside more or less prehistoric times and isolated survivals of these times such as Pythagoreanism and Nordic art.

11. "Without knowledge of the science of dancing it is hard to understand the rules of painting" (*Vishnu-Dharma-Uttara*). "Only those sculptures or paintings should be judged beautiful which conform to canonical prescriptions, not those which please a personal taste of fantasy" (Shukracharya). "The particular form suitable to each image is to be found described in the *Shilpa-Shāstras*, the canonical texts followed by the image-makers. . . . These texts supply the data needed for the mental representation which serves as the sculptor's model. According to his vision, says Shukracharya, he will fashion in temples the image of the divinities he adores. It is thus, and not by some other means, in truth and not by direct observation, that he will be able to attain his goal. — The essential part of art, the "visualization" (and one could say the same of the ecstatic audition of the musician) is thus a kind of yoga; the artist is sometimes looked on as a sort of yogi. Often, before undertaking his work, he celebrates certain special rites aimed at stifling the working of

moral nor immoral, for the Hindu sees in sexual matters their essential cosmic or divine aspect and not their accidental physical aspect.[12] Hindu architecture also has a foundation in the Scriptures, which describe its celestial origin; its profound connection with Hindu dancing results from the form of the Vedic sacrifice.[13] The whole of Hindu architecture is essentially a coordination of the circle and the square in accord with the Vedic fire altar, Agni; in other words the architecture is derived from the primordial altar.[14]

If there is something vegetative, and thus alive, about the Hindu temple because of this sort of spiritualized sensuality characterizing the Hindu soul — a sensuality always close to asceticism and death and opening on to the Infinite —

the conscious will and setting free the subjective faculties. In this case truth does not come from visual observation but from "muscular awareness" of the movements the artist has understood and realized in his own members. — The Shastras also give the canons of proportion. These proportions vary according to the divinity to be represented. Architecture also has its own canons which regulate even the very smallest details" (A. Coomaraswamy: *Understanding Hindu Art*).

12. The average Westerner is always ready to reproach Hindus for what he believes to be "impurity"; for a true Hindu it is this very reproach that shows an impure attitude.

13. "It is hardly necessary to point out that the Vedic sacrifice, which is always described as the imitation of "what was at the beginning," is, in all its forms and in the full meaning of the terms, a work of art and at the same time a synthesis of the arts of liturgy and architecture, and one can say the same of the Christian Mass (which is also a sacrifice in mime) where the dramatic and architectural elements are inseparably united" (A. Coomaraswamy: The Nature of "Folklore" and "Popular Art" in *Christian and Oriental Philosophy of Art*, New York, 1956).

14. Hindu cosmology concerning the cardinal points and architecture coincides remarkably with that of the North American Indians, and also to some extent with that of the peoples of Siberia, so that it is easy to see in this fact a same heritage from the Hyperborean tradition. The circle appears again in the form of the Red Indian's camp surrounding the central fire, as also in the form of their tents or huts, while the symbolism of the square is actualized in the rite of the Sacred Pipe.

Greek and Egyptian temples mark, each in their own way, an opposite point of view. The Greek temple relates to a perspective of wisdom marked by a clarity which is no doubt already too rational; it indicates measure and the logical finite. The use of marble and the choice of profane subjects went hand in hand with the decadence of Greek statuary which originally used wood and metal and represented only the Gods. As for the Egyptian temple, it stands, not "in space" like the Greek temple, but "in eternity"; it suggests the mystery of the Immutable and gives the impression of being of the same order as the starry vault of heaven.

Christian art for its part is founded, from a doctrinal point of view, on the mystery of the Son, "Image" of the Father, or the mystery of God "become man" (or image) in order that man (made in the image of God) might "become God." In this art the central element is painting: tradition says that it goes back to the likeness of Christ miraculously imprinted on a cloth sent to King Abgar, as also to the portrait of the Virgin Mary painted by St. Luke; another archetype of icons of the Blessed Face is, by its very nature, the Holy Shroud, prototype of the sacred portraits, and then the Crucifix. The Seventh Oecumenical Council declared that "the painting of icons was in no wise an invention of painters, but is on the contrary an established institution and tradition of the Church."[15] But the general

15. In the sixteenth century the Patriarch Nikon ordered the destruction of icons influenced by the Renaissance and threatened with excommunication those who painted or owned such paintings. After him the Patriarch Joachim required — in his last will and testament — that icons should always be painted according to ancient models and not "follow Latin or German models, which are invented according to the personal whim of the artist and corrupt the tradition of the Church." Many texts of this kind could be cited. In India, tradition speaks of the painter Chitrakara who was cursed by a brahmin for having broken the rules in the composition of a painting for which he had received a commission. If painted pictures are a necessary expression of Christian spirituality, sculptured images have only a secondary necessity which is also more or less

use of icons was not imposed without difficulty: if the early Christians had some difficulty in admitting them this was by reason of the Judaic heritage; their scruples were of the same order as those of the Jewish-born Christians over abandoning the Mosaic prescriptions about food. It is in the nature of certain traditional values that they are only actualized fully in a particular human situation; in the realm of sacred art the doctrine of St. John Damascene was providential because it formulated truths which could not have been enunciated in the earliest days of Christianity.

Sacred art also has fields which are more or less secondary, not by definition, but from the point of view of a particular traditional perspective — in Christianity, for example, architecture and enamel work; and it often contains elements drawn from pre-existing art which provide the primary matter — up till then symbolically "in chaos" — for the new art: thus it was that the spiritual genius of Christianity was able to make use of Greco-Roman, Oriental and Nordic elements for its artistic expressions. Such elements were reforged into a powerful original mode of expression and the same can be said, *mutatis mutandis,* of the elements used by the Islamic and Buddhist civilizations.

The Buddhist conception of art is, at least in certain respects, not remote from the Christian: like Christian art, Buddhist art is centered on the image of the Superman,

---

"local." A cathedral covered with sculpture is assuredly a profound and powerful expression of Christianity, but one that is essentially determined by a fusion of Teutonic with Latin genius. A Gothic facade aims at embodying a preaching as concretely as possible; it may include esoteric elements — and indeed must do so by reason of its symbolism — but it has not the quasi-sacramental character of an iconostasis, a character that Charlemagne misunderstood because of his typically Western "rationalism" according to which the purpose of pictures or images was merely didactic. One of the glories of the Western cathedral is its stained glass, which is like an opening towards heaven: the rose-window is like a sparkling symbol of the metaphysical universe, of the cosmic reverberations of the "Self."

bearer of the Revelation, though it differs from the Christian perspective in its non-theism, which brings everything back to the impersonal; if man is logically at the center of the cosmos, that is, for Buddhism, "by accident" and not from theological necessity as in the case of Christianity; persons are "ideas" rather than individuals. Buddhist art evolves round the sacramental image of the Buddha, given, according to one tradition, in the lifetime of the Blessed One in different forms, both sculptural and pictorial. The situation is the opposite of that of Christian art, for here statuary is more important than painting although the latter is nonetheless strictly canonical and not "discretionary" like Christian statuary. In the realm of architecture, we may mention the *stūpa* of Piprava built immediately after the death of Shakyamuni; apart from this, elements of Hindu and Chinese art were transmuted into a new art of which there were a number of variants both in the Theravada and the Mahayana schools. From a doctrinal point of view the art in this case is founded on the idea of the saving virtue emanating from the superhuman beauty of the Buddhas: the images of the Blessed One, of other Buddhas and of Bodhisattvas are sacramental crystallizations of this virtue, which is also manifested in cult objects, "abstract" as to their form but "concrete" in their nature. This principle furnishes a conclusive argument against profane religious art as practiced in the West, for the celestial beauty of the Man-God extends to the whole of traditional art, whatever the particular style required by a given collectivity; to deny traditional art — and here we have Christianity chiefly in mind — is to deny the saving beauty of the Word made flesh; it is to be ignorant of the fact that in true Christian art there is something of Christ and something of the Virgin. Profane art replaces the soul of the Man-God, or of the Perfected Man, by that of the artist and of his human model.

In Chinese art — setting aside Hindu influences in Buddhist art — everything seems to be derived, on the one hand from the writing, which has a sacred character, and on the other hand from nature, which is also sacred and is observed lovingly as a permanent revelation of Universal Principles. Certain techniques and materials — bronze, paper, Indian ink, lacquer, silk, bamboo and porcelain — contribute to the originality of this art and determine certain of its modes. The connection between calligraphy and painting is both close and decisive, a connection also to be found in Egyptian art. Writing is a form of painting; the Yellow people trace their characters with a brush and their painting holds a quality of writing; hand and eye retain the same reflexes. Of Confucianist painting it can be said that it is neither essentially sacred nor yet wholly profane; its intention is ethical in a very broad sense of that term; it tends to represent the "objective" innocence of things and not their inner reality. As for Taoist landscapes, these externalize a metaphysic and a contemplative state: they spring, not from space, but from the "void"; their theme is essentially "mountain and water" and with this they combine cosmological and metaphysical aims. It is one of the most powerfully original forms of sacred art; in a certain sense it stands at the antipodes of Hindu art in which the principle of expression is precision and rhythm and not the ethereal subtleties of a contemplation made up of imponderables. It is not surprising that *Chan* Buddhism (*Zen* in Japanese), whose character is at once unarticulated and rich in shades of meaning, should have found in Taoist art a congenial mode of expression.[16]

In architecture the major buildings of the Yellow race have the same superposed curves as the pines which sur-

16. In speaking of Chinese art we include also that of Japan which is a highly original branch of that art with its own particular spirit combining sobriety, boldness, elegance and contemplative intuition. The Japanese house combines the natural nobility of materials and simplicity of forms with extreme artistic refinement and this makes it one of the most original manifestations of art as a whole.

round them; the wide, horned and in a sense vegetative shape of the Far-Eastern roof — the whole usually resting on wooden columns — even if its prototype is not the sacred conifers, it nonetheless retraces their dynamic and majestic life. When a man of the Yellow race enters a temple or palace he enters a "forest" rather than a "cavern"[17]; this architecture has about it something living, something vegetative and warm; even the magical intention of the upward curved hips, which give the protecting roof a certain defensive aspect, bring us back to the connection between tree and lightning and so to virgin nature.[18]

The non-figurative or abstract arts of Judaism and Islam must not be overlooked. The former was revealed in the Torah itself and is exclusively sacerdotal. The latter is akin to it by its exclusion of human and animal representations; as to its origin, it issued from the sensory form of the revealed Book, that is, from the interlaced letters of the verses of the Koran, and also — paradoxical though this may seem — from the forbidding of images. This restriction in Islamic art, by eliminating certain creative possibilities intensified others, the more so since it was accompanied by express permission to represent plants; hence the capital importance of arabesques, of geometrical and botanical decorative

17. A Gothic cathedral is a petrified forest, in one way welcoming, though in another remaining cold; to the idea of protection it adds the idea of eternity and so mingles a celestial coldness with mercy. Its stained glass windows are like a sky glimpsed through the foliage of a forest of stone.

18. There is a story that the Chinese roof represents a boat upside down: according to a Sino-Malayan myth the sun comes from the East in a boat and the boat is wrecked in the West and, turning over, covers the sun, thus producing night; a connection is made, not only between the overturned boat and the darkness of night, but also, as a consequence, between a roof and the sleep it protects. Another source of Far-Eastern architecture, so far as the wooden columns are concerned, may be the primitive Sino-Malayan lake-dwellings. (See E. Fuhkmann: *China*, Hagen, 1921.)

motifs.[19] Islamic architecture, inherited from the neighboring civilizations, was transmuted by its own particular genius which tended at the same time both to simplification and to ornamentation; the purest expression of this genius is perhaps the art of the Maghreb, where no pre-existing formalism invited concessions. In Islam the love of beauty compensates for the tendency to austere simplicity; it lends elegant forms to simplicity and partially clothes it in a profusion of precious and abstract lacework. "God is Beautiful," said the Prophet, "and He loveth beauty."[20]

All that has just been said certainly does not mean that partial deviations may not arise in traditional art: especially in the case of the plastic arts it sometimes happens that a more or less superficial virtuosity stifles the clarity of the symbolism and the inner reality of the work; worldliness can lead to errors and faults of taste even in sacred art, although the hieratic quality of the latter reduces the danger of such deviations to a minimum.

19. Persian miniatures integrate things in a surface without perspective, and thus in a sense without limits, like a piece of weaving, and it is this which makes them compatible — at any rate as "worldly" objects — with the Islamic perspective. In a general way Moslems distrust any "materialization" of religious subjects as if in fear that spiritual realities might become exhausted through an excess of sensory crystallization. The sculptured and dramatic imagery of the Roman Church has indeed proven to be a two-edged sword; instead of making it "sensitive" and popular, the Church ought to have maintained in it the hieratic abstraction of Romanesque statuary. It is not the sole obligation of art to come down towards the common people; it should also remain faithful to its intrinsic truth in order to allow men to rise towards that truth.

20. It is understandable that the smiling grace of Islamic architecture should have appeared to many Christians as something worldly and "pagan"; indeed the volitive perspective envisages the here-below and the hereafter only as levels of existence which mark separation and opposition and not as universal essences which unite and make identical. In Renaissance art virtue becomes crushing, lugubrious and tiresome: beside the Alhambra the palace of Charles V seeks to be grave and austere but only achieves a heaviness and opacity which banish all higher intelligence, contemplation and serenity.

After these very summary considerations let us return to the purely technical aspects of art. It is important to make a distinction between intentional stylization and mere individual lack of skill, evidenced either by an opacity introduced into the style or by an impression of unintelligence, embarrassment and arbitrariness. In other words, it is necessary to know how to differentiate between an "artlessness" which, in transmitting positive suggestions, becomes thereby precious, and faults due to the personal incompetence or coarseness of the artisan. An apparent fault in drawing may arise from an intuition of harmony and may contribute to beauty of expression, of composition, of equilibrium; precision of drawing may be subordinated to other more important qualities to the extent that the content is spiritual. Apart from this, if traditional art cannot be always and everywhere at a peak of attainment, this is not because of any principial insufficiency but because of man's intellectual and moral insufficiencies which cannot fail to become exteriorized in art as in his other activities.

The agreement of a picture with nature is legitimate only insofar as it does not abolish the separation between the work of art and its outward model; without such separation the former loses its sufficient reason, for its purpose is not merely to repeat what already exists; the exactness of its proportions must neither do violence to the material — the plane surface in the case of painting and the inert material in the case of sculpture — nor compromise the spiritual expression; if the correctness of the proportions is in accord with the material data of the particular art while also satisfying the spiritual intention of the work, it will add an expression of intelligence and so also of truth to the symbolism of the work. Authentic and normative art always tends to combine intelligent observation of nature with noble and profound stylizations in order, first, to assimilate the work to the model created by God in nature and, secondly, to separate it from physical contingency by giving it an imprint of pure spirit, of synthesis, of what is essential. It can definitely be said that naturalism is legitimate insofar as physical exactness is allied to a vision of the Platonic Idea, the qualitative archetype; hence, in such works, the predominance of the static, of symmetry, of the essential.[21] But we must also take account of this: if we start out from the idea that form is in a way necessarily opposed to essence, the latter being universal inwardness and the former "accidental" outwardness, we can explain certain deformations practiced in sacred art as a reduction to the essence or as a "scorching by the essence," so to speak. The essence will then appear as an inner fire which disfigures, or as an "abyss" in which proportions are shattered, so that what is sacred and "formless" (in the spiritual, not in the chaotic sense) is like an irruption of essence into form.

Again, it is important not to lose sight of the fact that the human spirit cannot be simultaneously deployed in all directions. Since traditional symbolism by no means implies by definition an observation of physical forms carried to extreme lengths there is no reason for a sacerdotal art to tend towards such observation; it will be content with what the natural genius of the race requires, and this explains that mixture of "deforming" symbolism and refined observation which characterizes sacred art in general. At times the qualitative aspect does violence to the quantitative reality: Hindu art marks femininity by the breasts and hips and gives them the importance of ideograms; it transforms into symbols characteristics which would otherwise simply be

21. In this connection Egyptian art is particularly instructive; other examples of this coincidence of "natural" and "essential" can be found in Far-Eastern art and also in the admirable bronze and pottery heads found among the Yorubas of Ife in West Africa which are among the most perfect works of art to be found anywhere.

accepted as natural facts, and this is related to the "deforming essence" mentioned above. As for simple lack of physical observation, which as such is independent of any
symbolical intention, we would add that, where it is condi-
tioned by the requirements of a particular collective soul, it
is an integral part of a style and so of a language which is in
itself intelligent and noble; this is something quite different
from the technical clumsiness of some isolated artist. Complete naturalism, which reproduces the chance variations
and accidental aspect of appearances, is truly an abuse of
intelligence such as might be called "luciferian"[22]: it could
not, therefore, characterize traditional art. Moreover, if the
difference between a naturalistic drawing and a stylized but
unskillful drawing, or that between a flat and decorative
painting and another in which there are shadows and perspective, represented progress pure and simple, this progress would be enormous and also inexplicable because of its
very enormity. If one were to suppose that the Greeks —
and after them the Christians — had been for many centuries incapable of looking and drawing, how could one then
explain that these same men became endowed with ability
to look and draw after a lapse of time that was relatively very
short? This easy change between incommensurable positions proves that there was here no real progress and that
on the contrary naturalism only represents a more exteriorized outlook combined with the efforts of observation and
skill called for by this new way of viewing things.

The whole of the so-called "Greek miracle" amounts to
a substitution of reason alone for intelligence as such; apart
from the rationalism which inaugurated it, artistic natural-

---

22. This abuse of intelligence is extremely characteristic of modern
civilization. Many things are taken to be superior — as indeed they are if
considered in artificial isolation — which are in fact merely hypertrophic;
artistic naturalism is just that, at any rate when taken as an end in itself
and when it consequently expresses nothing more than the limitations of
form and of the accidental.

ism would have been inconceivable. Extreme naturalism results from the cult of "form," of form envisaged as something finite and not as "symbol"; reason indeed regulates the science of the finite, of limits and of order, so that it is only logical that an art which is directed by reason should share with reason itself a flatness refractory to all mystery. The art of classical antiquity is often compared to the brightness of full daylight; it is forgotten that it also has the "outward" quality of daylight, which lacks any aspect of the secret and the infinite. From the standpoint of this rationalistic ideal, the art of the cathedrals — and also Asiatic art, to the extent that it was known — inevitably appears chaotic, "disorderly," irrational and inhuman.

Now, if we start from the idea that perfect art can be recognized by three main criteria: nobility of content — this being a spiritual condition apart from which art has no right to exist — then exactness of symbolism or at least, in the case of profane works of art, harmony of composition,[23] and finally purity of style or elegance of line and color, we can discern with the help of these criteria the qualities and defects of any work of art whether sacred or not. It goes without saying that some modern work may, as if by chance, possess these qualities; nonetheless it would be a mistake to see in this any justification of an art that is deprived of all positive principles; the exceptional qualities of such a work are in any case far from being characteristic of the art in question when viewed as a whole, but appear only incidentally under cover of the eclecticism which goes with anarchy. The existence of such works proves, however, that a legitimate profane art is conceivable in the West without any need to return purely and simply to the miniatures of the Middle Ages or to peasant

23. This condition equally requires correct measure in regard to size; a profane work should never exceed certain dimensions; those are, for miniatures, very small.

painting,[24] for a healthy state of soul and a normal treatment of materials always guarantee the rectitude of an art devoid of pretensions. It is the nature of things — on the spiritual and on the psychological as well as on the material and technical level — which demands that each of the constituent elements of art should fulfill certain elementary conditions, these being precisely the ones by which all traditional art is governed.

Here it is important to point out that one of the major errors of modern art is its confusion of art materials: people no longer know how to distinguish the cosmic significance of stone, iron and wood, just as they do not know the objective qualities of forms and colors. Stone has this in common with iron that it is cold and implacable, whereas wood is warm, live and kindly; but, while the coldness of stone is neutral and indifferent like that of eternity, iron is hostile, aggressive and ill-natured, and this enables us to understand the significance of the invasion of the world by iron.[25] The heavy and sinister nature of iron requires that in its use in handicrafts it should be treated with lightness and fantasy such as one sees for instance in old church screens which resemble lacework. The wickedness of iron

---

24. Obviously the same cannot be said insofar as sacred art is concerned; in the West this is exclusively the art of icons and cathedrals and has by definition a character of immutability. Here let us once again mention the popular art of various European countries, which is, at least in a relative sense, Nordic in origin, though it is difficult to assign a precise origin to an art of immemorial antiquity. This "rustic" art, preserved chiefly among the Germanic peoples and Slavs, has moreover no clear geographical limits and certain of its fundamental motifs can be traced even into Africa and Asia, though in the latter case there is no need to presume any borrowing. Here is a most perfect art and one which is in principle capable of bringing health to the chaos in which what remains of our craftsmen are floundering.

25. The accumulation in Christian churches and places of pilgrimage of gross and harsh iron work cannot but impede the radiation of spiritual forces. It always gives the impression that heaven is imprisoned.

ought to be neutralized by transparence in its treatment, for this does no violence to the nature of this metal but on the contrary confers legitimacy on its qualities of hardness and inflexibility; the sinister nature of iron implies that it has no right to full and direct manifestation but should be harshly treated or broken in order to be able to express its virtues. The nature of stone is quite different; in the raw state it has something sacred about it, and this is also true of the noble metals, which are like iron transfigured by light or cosmic fire or by planetary forces. It must be added that concrete — which, like iron, has invaded the whole world — is a base and quantitative sort of counterfeit stone; in it the spiritual aspect of eternity is replaced by an anonymous and brutal heaviness; if stone is implacable like death, concrete is brutal like destruction.

Before proceeding further we would wish to add the following reflection, not unrelated to the expansion of iron and its tyranny: one may be astonished at the haste shown by the most artistic peoples of the East in adopting ugly things of the modern world; but it must not be forgotten that, apart from any question of aesthetics or spirituality, people have in all ages imitated those who were strongest: before having strength people want to have at least the appearance of strength, and the ugly things of the modern world have become synonymous with power and independence. The essence of artistic beauty is spiritual, whereas material strength is "worldly," and since the worldly regard strength as synonymous with intelligence, the beauty of the tradition becomes synonymous not merely with weakness, but also with stupidity, illusion and the ridiculous; being ashamed of weakness is almost always accompanied by hatred of what is looked on as the cause of this apparent inferiority — in this case, tradition, contemplation, truth. If most people — regardless of social level — unfortunately have not enough discernment to overcome this lamentable optical illusion, some salutary reactions are nonetheless observable in some quarters.

*

* *

It is told of Til Eulenspiegel[26] that, having been engaged as court painter to a prince, he presented to the assembled company a blank canvas, declaring that whoever was not the child of honest parents would see nothing on the canvas. Since none of the assembled lords was willing to admit he saw nothing, all pretended to admire the blank canvas. Now there was a time when this tale could pass as a pleasantry but none would have dared to foretell that it would one day enter into the manners of a "civilized" world. But in our day a nobody can in the name of art for art's sake show us anything he likes[27] and, if we cry out in protest in the name of truth and intelligence, we are told we have not understood, as though some mysterious deficiency prevented us from understanding, not Chinese or Aztec art, but some inferior daub by a European living in the next street. According to an abuse of language very prevalent today "to understand" means "to accept" and to reject means not to understand, as if it never happened that one refuses something precisely because one does understand it or on the contrary that one accepts it because one does not.

Behind all this lies a double and fundamental error but for which the pretensions of so-called artists would be inconceivable: namely that an originality counter to the hereditary collective norm is psychologically possible outside mental derangement and that a man can produce a true work of art which is not in any degree understandable to a great many intelligent and cultivated people belonging to the same civilization, the same race and the same period

26. A character of medieval legend, famous for his pranks.
27. The author is here thinking chiefly of the West (Translator's note).

as the self-styled artist.[28] In reality the premises of such originality or singularity do not exist in the normal human soul; still less do they exist in pure intelligence. Modern peculiarities, far from relating to some "mystery" of artistic creation, are merely philosophical error and mental deformity. Everyone believes himself obliged to be a great man; novelty is taken for originality, morbid introspection for profundity, cynicism for sincerity and pretentiousness for genius, so that a point is even reached where a diagram of microbes or some zebra-like striping may be accepted as a painting. "Sincerity" is elevated to the rank of an absolute criterion, as though a work of art could not be psychologically sincere and at the same time spiritually false or artistically a nullity. Artists so affected make the grave mistake of deliberately ignoring the objective and qualitative value of forms and colors and of believing themselves to be sheltered in a subjectivism which they deem interesting and impenetrable, whereas in reality it is merely commonplace and ridiculous. Their very mistake forces them to have recourse to the lowest possibilities in the world of forms, just as Satan, in wishing to be as "original" as God, had no choice open to him but the abominable.[29] In a general way cynicism seems to play an important part in a certain atheistical morality: virtue, it says, consists not in dominating oneself and remaining silent, but in letting oneself run riot and proclaiming the fact from every housetop; every sin is

28. This is singularity carried to its limit, to the point of caricature. Now it is well known that "singularity" is a defect stigmatized by every monastic discipline; its gravity is related to the sin of pride.

29. Modern art builds misshapen churches and pierces their walls with asymmetrical windows looking like the results of bursts of machine-gun fire, as if by this means to betray its own true feelings. However much people may boast of the boldness of some such architectural design, they cannot escape the intrinsic meaning of forms: they cannot prevent such a work from being related by the language of its forms to the world of phantoms and nightmares: this is spiritualism transmuted into reinforced concrete.

good if boasted of with brutality; a struggle in silence is labeled "hypocrisy" because something remains concealed. To the same order of ideas belongs the belief that it is "sincere" or "realistic" to uncover cynically what nature keeps hidden as though nature acted without sufficient reason.

The modern conception of art is false insofar as it puts creative imagination — or even simply the impulse to create — in the place of qualitative form, or insofar as a subjective and conjectural valuation is substituted for an objective and spiritual one; to do this is to replace by talent alone — by talent real or illusory — that skill and craftsmanship which must needs enter into the very definition of art, as if talent could have meaning apart from the normative constants that are its criteria. It is clear that originality has no meaning except through its content, exactly as is the case with sincerity; the originality of an error or the talent of an incompetent and subversive individual could not offer the slightest interest: a well-executed copy of a good model is worth more than an original creation which is the "sincere" manifestation of an evil genius.[30] When everyone wants to create and no one is willing to copy; when every work wants to be unique instead of inserting itself into a traditional continuity from which it draws its sap and of which it eventually may become one of the finest flowers, it only remains for man to cry out his own nothingness in the face of the world; this nothingness will of course be viewed as synonymous with originality since the minimum of tradition or normality will be taken for a maximum of talent. In the same order of ideas let us also mention the prejudice

30. It often happens that the value of a work is denied because someone has discovered — or thinks he has — that it had been wrongly ascribed, as if the value of a work of art lay outside itself. In traditional art the masterpiece is most often an anonymous culmination of a series of replicas; a work of genius is almost always the resultant of a long collective elaboration. For example, many Chinese masterpieces are copies of which the models are unknown.

which would require every artist to "make himself anew," as though human life were not far too short to justify such a requirement or as though artists were not sufficiently numerous to render such a renewal on the part of each of them superfluous. After all one does not complain of the fact that a man's face remains the same from day to day, nor does one expect Persian art to turn suddenly into Polynesian art.

The error in the thesis of "art for art's sake" really amounts to supposing that these are relativities which bear their adequate justification within themselves, in their own relative nature, and that consequently there are criteria of value inaccessible to pure intelligence and foreign to objective truth. This error involves abolishing the primacy of the spirit and its replacement either by instinct or taste, thus by criteria that are either purely subjective or else arbitrary. We have already seen that the definition, laws and criteria of art cannot be derived from art itself, that is, from the competence of the artist as such; the foundations of art lie in the spirit, in metaphysical, theological and mystical knowledge, not in knowledge of the craft alone nor yet in genius, for this may be just anything; in other words the intrinsic principles of art are essentially subordinate to extrinsic principles of a higher order. Art is an activity, an exteriorization, and thus depends by definition on a knowledge that transcends it and gives it order; apart from such knowledge, art has no justification: it is knowledge which determines action, manifestation, form, and not the reverse. It is not necessary to produce works of art oneself in order to have the right to judge an artistic production in its essentials; decisive artistic competence only comes into play in relation to an intellectual competence which must be already present.[31] No relative point of view can claim

---

31. This competence may, however, be limited to a particular traditional world. The competence of a brahmin may not extend to Christian icons, though there is here no limitation of principle. A necessary com-

unqualified competence except in the case of innocuous activities in which competence anyhow has but a very limited importance; now human art derives from a relative point of view; it is an application, not a principle.

Modern criticism more and more tends to put works of art into factitious categories: art is thus made out to be no more than a movement, and a point has been reached where works of art are appraised only in terms of other works and apart from any objective and stable criterion. The artist of the "*avant-garde*" is one whose vanity and cynicism impart momentum to the movement; critics seek, not for works which are good in themselves — some of them would deny that such works exist — but for works which are novel or "sincere" and can serve as points of reference in a movement which is in reality a downhill slide towards dissolution; the quality of art is then seen only in its movement and its relationships, which amounts to saying that no work has intrinsic value; everything has become fugitive and discontinuous. Artistic relativism destroys the very notion of art just as philosophical relativism destroys the notion of truth; relativism of whatever kind kills intelligence. One who despises truth cannot in sound logic propound his own contempt of it as truth.

In the same context it is significant that people are quite ready to extol some so-called artist on the ground that he "expresses his period" as though a period as such — something which may have no particular character — had rights over truth;[32] if what a "surrealist" expresses really corresponded to our times, this expression would prove only one thing, namely, that our times are not worth expressing; very

petence has the right, though not of course the duty, to be limited to a particular system of concordant possibilities.

32. This compliment is even paid to philosophers; "the existential," the bare fact, everywhere crushes what is true by taking its name. "The contemporary period" is a sort of false divinity in whose name everything seems permissible, whether on the plane of thought, or that of art, even religious art.

fortunately, however, our times do still contain something besides surrealism. Be that as it may, to claim that a work of art is good because "it expresses our times" amounts to affirming that a phenomenon is good simply because it expresses something; in that case crime is good because it expresses a criminal tendency, an error is good because it expresses a lack of knowledge and so forth. What defenders of surrealist tendencies either forget or do not know is above all that forms, whether in pictures, in sculpture, in architecture or in some other medium, arise from a hierarchy of cosmic values and translate either truths or errors so that there is no place here for adventuring; the psychological efficacy of forms, so beneficial when they are true, makes them on the contrary deadly if they are false.

In order to maintain an illusion of objectivity with a shifting subjectivity, imaginary and definitely hysterical qualities are projected into the most insignificant futilities: people discuss endlessly about "shades of contrast and balance" as if these were not to be found everywhere; in doing so they end by trampling in scorn rugs which are masterpieces of abstract art though unsigned. When almost anything may be art and anyone may be an artist, neither the word "art" nor the word "artist" retains any meaning; it is true that there exists a perversion of sensibility and intelligence ready to discover new dimensions and even "drama" in the most uncalled for extravagances, but a sane man has no need to occupy his mind with these things.[33] The great mistake of the surrealists is to believe that profundity lies in the direction of what is individual, that it is this, and not the universal, which is mysterious, and that the mystery grows more profound the more one delves into what is obscure and morbid: this is mystery turned upside

---

33. One can find "abstract" works — though not commonly — which are neither better nor worse than some African shield, but why then make celebrities of their authors, or why not, on the other hand, count every Zulu as one of the "giants" of art?

down and therefore satanic, and it is at the same time a counterfeit of the "originality" — or uniqueness — of God. The error is to be found, however, also on another and seemingly opposite side: art then becomes an uninspired technique and a work of art amounts to no more than a "construction"; there it is not a case of residues of the subconscious, but only of reason and calculation, though this by no means excludes interferences from the irrational any more than intuitive surrealism excludes calculated procedures. Pseudo-sincere affectations of simplicity do not escape from this same condemnation, for brutal compression and idiotism have nothing to do with the simplicity of primordial things.

All that has been said above also applies moreover both to poetry and to music: here again some people arrogate to themselves the right to call realistic or sincere anything which, they say, "expresses the spirit of our age," when the reality to which they refer is only a factitious world from which they can no longer escape: they make a virtue of this incapacity and then disdainfully apply the label of "romanticism" or "nostalgia" to the innate need for harmony which is proper to every normal man. Ultramodern music — "electronic music" for example — is founded on a despising of everything that enters into the very definition of music; *mutatis mutandis*, the case of the poetic art is similar: it becomes no more than a system of sounds — most miserably fabricated — which violates the principle at the basis of poetry. There is no possible justification for this puerile mania for "making a clean sweep" of centuries or millennia in order to "start from scratch," to invent new "principles," new bases, new structures, for such invention is not merely senseless in itself but also incompatible with any creative sincerity. In other words some things are mutually exclusive: no one can call forth a poem from his heart while at the same time inventing out of nothing a language in which to express it. Here, as with the visual arts, the initial error is belief in a quasi-absolute originality, that is, in something which does not answer to any positive possibility, the musical sense of a racial or traditional collectivity not being capable of a modification extending to its very roots.[34] People talk about liberating music from this or that prejudice, or convention, or constraint; what they really do is to "liberate" it from its own nature just as they have "liberated" painting from painting, poetry from poetry and architecture from architecture; surrealism has "freed" art from art just as by execution a body has been freed from life.

This allusion to music obliges us to draw attention to the fact that at the time of the Renaissance and in the following centuries the decadence of European music and poetry was incomparably less — if indeed there was any decadence or to the extent there was — than that of the plastic arts and of architecture; there is no common measure between the sonnets of Michaelangelo and the works for which he is more famous,[35] or between Shakespeare or Palestrina and the visual art of their day. The music of the Renaissance,

34. We have heard certain Asiatic music blamed for its "simplistic method," and this is characteristic of a mental deformation which admires only what is factitious or forced: everything is shut up in a psychosis of "work," of "creation," even of "construction," factors which became synonymous with "quality" as though the beauty of a flower or a bird's song depended on laborious and hypercritical research, on an atmosphere of laboratories and vivisection.

35. Apart from his sonnets the human greatness of Michaelangelo appears chiefly in his sculpture, in works like the *Moses* and the *Pieta*, and that apart from any question of principles or style. In his painting and architecture this greatness is as if crushed by the errors of the period; it gets lost in heaviness and pathos or in the cold gigantism that also characterizes the statues and which is a dominant mark of the Renaissance. With the impressionists the academic spirit fell into discredit; one would gladly believe that this was due to a slightly deeper understanding, but such is not the case, for an unforeseeable change of fashion was enough to call everything once again into question; moreover the academical spirit has already been revived within surrealism, though always in the climate of the oppressive ugliness characteristic of that school.

like that of the Middle Ages of which it is a continuation, expresses in sound what is great and chivalrous in the European soul; it makes one think of wine or mead and of stirring legends of the past. The reason for this disproportion between the arts is that intellectual decadence — decadence of contemplative, not of inventive intelligence — is far more directly manifested in the visual arts, in which elements of intellectuality are strongly involved, than in auditive or "iterative" arts, which chiefly exteriorize the many and various states — and ultimately the beauties — of that plastic substance which is the soul.[36] In the plastic arts and in architecture the Renaissance means an art of passion and megalomania; the baroque, is an art of dreams. In music, baroque exteriorizes what may be lovable, tender or paradisal in the dream, whereas in the visual arts it manifests the illusory and ludicrous aspects, enchantment coagulating into a nightmare. In the nineteenth century romantic poetry and music reinforced and made more acute the attachments to earth; like all sentimental individualism, this was a terrible sowing of agonies and sorrows, though in romanticism in the widest sense there are still many beauties one would wish to see integrated into a love of God.

Whereas ancient music included a spiritual value which can still be felt even in music of the end of the eighteenth century, the plane of music changed at the start of the nineteenth century so that it became in fact a kind of substitute for religion or mysticism: more than in the pro-

---

36. English architecture was less devastated by the Renaissance and by baroque than that of most continental countries. It may be that, by one of those paradoxes of which history is prodigal, Anglicanism preserved, (against Rome) a certain medieval heritage in matters of art, and this would seem to have been the less unlikely since the English are less creative than the Italians, Germans or French. Something analogous could no doubt be said about the popular architecture of Spain and particularly of Andalusia where Arab influence seems to have played the part of a preserver.

fane music of the preceding periods musical emotion came to assume the function of an irrational excuse for every human frailty; music grew ever more hypersensitive and grandiloquent to the degree that everyday life became imbued with scientific rationalism and mercantile materialism. But in general it was still real music, linked with cosmic qualities and consequently capable of becoming, even if rarely, the vehicle of a movement of the soul towards Heaven.

Let us, however, return to the plastic arts and add the following, which will at the same time serve as a conclusion: for contemporary artists and insofar as profane art is concerned, there can be no question of just "going back," for one never gets back to one's starting point; rather should the valid experiments of naturalism and impressionism be combined with the principles of normal and normalizing art as is in fact done by some artists who are in general little known; modern art — starting from the Renaissance — does include some more or less isolated works which, though they fit into the style of their period, are in a deeper sense opposed to it and neutralize its errors by their own qualities.[37] However, in the case of sacred art resort to canonical models and treatment is called for without reservation, for if there is in modern man an originality to which a human being may have a right, this will not fail to show

---

37. Of famous or well-known painters the elder Brueghel's snow scenes may be quoted and, nearer to our day, Gauguin, some of whose canvases are almost perfect, Van Gogh's flower paintings, Douanier Rousseau with his exotic forests akin to folk painting, and, among our contemporaries, Covarrubias with his Mexican and Balinese subjects. We might perhaps also allude to certain American Indian painters whose work shows, through a naturalistic influence, a vision close to that of the ancient pictography. Conversely, equivalents of the positive experiments of modern art can be found in the most varied of traditional art, which proves not only that these experiments are compatible with the universal principles of art, but also that — once again — "there is nothing new under the sun."

itself within the framework of tradition, as already happened in the Middle Ages according to the diverse mentalities in space and time. But above all, it is necessary to relearn how to see and to look, and to understand that the sacred belongs to the field of the immutable and not to that of change; it is not a question of tolerating a certain artistic stability on the basis of a pretended law of change, but on the contrary of tolerating a certain variation on the basis of the necessary and clear immutability of the sacred; it is not enough that there be genius, it must also have a right to exist. Words such as "conformism" and "immobilism" have been coined so as to be able to escape with good conscience from everything which, in the formal clothing of Revelation, necessarily participates in Immutability.

Insofar as profane art can be legitimate — and it can be, more than ever before, in this period of disfigurement and vulgarity — its mission is one of transmitting qualities of intelligence, beauty and nobility; and this is something which cannot be realized apart from the rules which are imposed on us, not only by the very nature of the art in question, but also by the spiritual truth flowing from the divine prototype of every human creation.

The Meaning of Caste

Like all other sacred institutions the system of castes is founded on the nature of things or, to be more exact, on one aspect of that nature, and thus on a reality which in certain circumstances cannot but manifest itself; this statement is equally valid as regards the opposite aspect, that of the equality of men before God. In short, in order to justify the system of castes it is enough to ask the following question: does diversity of qualifications and of heredity exist? If it does, then the system of castes is both possible and legitimate. In the case of an absence of castes, where this is traditionally imposed, the sole question is: are men equal, not just from the point of view of their animality which is not in question, but from the point of view of their final end? Since every man has an immortal soul this is certain; therefore in a given traditional society this consideration can take precedence over that of diversity of qualifications. The immortality of the soul is the postulate of religious "egalitarianism," just as the quasi-divine character of the intellect — and hence of the intellectual elite — is the postulate of the caste system.

One could not imagine any greater divergence than that between the hierarchical system of Hinduism and the leveling outlook of Islam, yet there is here only a difference of emphasis, for truth is one: indeed, if Hinduism considers first of all in human nature those fundamental tendencies which divide men into so many hierarchical categories, it

113

nevertheless realizes equality in the super-caste of wandering monks, the *sannyāsīs*, in which social origin no longer plays any part. The case of the Christian clergy is analogous in the sense that among them titles of nobility disappear: a peasant cannot become a prince, but he can become Pope and crown an Emperor. Conversely, some form of hierarchy appears even in the most "egalitarian" religions: in Islam, where every man is his own priest, the Sherifs, descendants of the Prophet, form a religious nobility and are thus superimposed on the rest of society, though without assuming in it any exclusive function. In the Christian world a citizen of note might be ennobled, whereas in the Hindu system such a thing is altogether excluded, because there the essential object of the higher castes is the maintenance of a primordial perfection; it is the descending sense given to the origin of castes that explains why caste can be lost but not acquired.[1] Indeed this perspective of "hereditary maintenance" is the very key to the caste system: it also explains the exclusiveness of admission to Hindu temples — the temples are not pulpits for preaching — and in a more general way the preponderant part played by rules of purity. The "obsession" of Hinduism is not the conversion of unbelievers, but on the contrary the maintaining of a primordial purity which is as much intellectual as moral and ritual.

What are the fundamental tendencies of human nature to which castes are more or less directly related? They could be defined as so many different ways of envisaging an empirical reality: in other words, the fundamental tendency in a man is connected with his "feeling" or "consciousness"

---

1. The late Pandit Hari Prasad Shastri did, however, assure us that there could be exceptions to this rule, quite apart from the possible reintegration of a family through successive marriages, and cited the case of King Vishvamitra, companion of Rama. In that case one should no doubt take into account the quality of the cyclic period and the special conditions created by the proximity of an *avatāra* of Vishnu.

of what is "real." For the *brāhmana* — the purely intellectual, contemplative and sacerdotal type — it is the changeless, the transcendent which is real; in his innermost heart he does not believe either in "life" or in "earth"; something in him remains foreign to change and to matter; broadly speaking such is his inner disposition — what might be called his "imaginative life" — whatever may be the personal weaknesses by which it is obscured. The *kshatriya* — the "knightly" type — has a keen intelligence, but it is turned towards action and analysis rather than towards contemplation and synthesis; his strength lies especially in his character; he makes up for the aggressiveness of his energy by his generosity and for his passionate nature by his nobility, self-control and greatness of soul. For this human type it is action that is "real," for it is by action that things are determined, modified and ordered; without action there is neither virtue nor honor nor glory. In other words the *kshatriya* believes in the efficacy of action rather than in the fatedness of a given situation: he despises the tyranny of facts and thinks only of determining their order, of clarifying a chaos, of cutting Gordian knots. Thus, just as for the *brāhmana* all is in motion and unreal except the Eternal and whatever is attached to It — truth, knowledge, contemplation, ritual, the Path — so for the *kshatriya* all is uncertain and peripheral except the constants of his *dharma* — action, honor, virtue, glory, nobility — on which for him all other values depend. This perspective can be transposed onto the religious plane without any essential change in its psychological quality.

For the *vaishya* — the merchant, the peasant, the artisan, the man whose activities are directly bound up with material values not merely *de facto* and accidentally but by virtue of his inner nature — it is riches, security, prosperity and well-being that are "real"; in his instinctive life other values are secondary and in his innermost heart he does not believe in them; his imagination expands on the plane of economic stability, of the material perfection of work and

115

the return it yields, and when this is transposed on to the religious plane it becomes exclusively a perspective of accumulating merit with a view to posthumous security. Outwardly this mentality is analogous to that of the *brāhmana* by reason of its static and pacific character; but it is remote from the mentality both of the *brāhmana* and the *kshatriya* because of a certain "narrowness" of the intelligence and will;[2] the *vaishya* is clever and possesses common sense, but he lacks specifically intellectual qualities and also chivalrous virtues, idealism in the higher sense of the term. Here it must be repeated that we are speaking, not of "classes," but of "castes," or, to be more precise, of "natural castes," since institutions as such, though they retrace nature, are never wholly free from the imperfections and vicissitudes of all manifestation. One does not belong to a particular caste because one follows a certain profession and is the issue of certain parents, but — at any rate under normal conditions — one follows a particular profession because one belongs to a certain caste and the latter is largely — though not absolutely — guaranteed by heredity; at least this guarantee is sufficient to render the Hindu system possible. This system has never been able to exclude exceptions, which

2. In the nineteenth century the bourgeois laity in Europe had for reasons of equilibrium to realize in their turn the qualities of the classes that had been eliminated; we are not referring here to the fact of belonging to the bourgeois class, which is in itself unimportant, but to the bourgeois spirit, which is quite a different thing. The preoccupation with science in the nineteenth and twentieth centuries, proves, not indeed that humanity has progressed, but that the "intellectuality" of men of mercantile type is hardly able to rise above the level of mere facts. The current illusion that man can rejoin metaphysical realities by dint of scientific discoveries is quite characteristic of this heaviness of spirit and only goes to prove that, as Guénon wrote, "the rise of the *vaishyas* spells intellectual night." Moreover "civilization," without any qualifying epithet and taken as *the* civilization, is a typically *vaishya* concept, and this explains on the one hand the current hatred for all that is considered "fanatical" and on the other hand an element of extreme affectation which forms a part of the oppressive system of the civilization in question.

as such confirm the rule; the fact that the exceptions have attained the largest possible number in our days of overpopulation and of the "realization of impossibilities" could not in any case vitiate the principle of hereditary hierarchy.

The "twice-born" (*dvīja*), namely the three castes of which we have spoken, might be defined as a spirit endowed with a body, and the *shūdra*, who represents the fourth caste, as a body endowed with human consciousness; in fact the *shūdra* is the man who is properly qualified only for manual work of a more of less quantitative kind and not for work demanding greater initiative and broader, more complex aptitudes; for this human type, which is still more widely separated from the preceding types than is the *vaishya* from the noble castes, it is bodily things that are "real"; it is eating and drinking which in this case strictly constitute happiness, these and their psychological concomitances;[3] in the innate perspective of the *shūdra*, in his "heart," all that lies outside the realm of bodily satisfaction smacks of luxury, not to say of "illusion," or in any case seems something "alongside" of what his imagination takes for reality, namely the satisfaction of immediate physical needs. It might be objected that the knightly type is also a pleasure-seeker, but this is not the point; here the question is above all the psychological function of enjoyment, the part it plays in an assemblage of compossibles; the *kshatriya* readily turns poet or aesthete, he lays very little stress on matter as such. The central and at the same time elementary place held by enjoyment in the innate perspective of the *shūdra* explains his often carefree, dissipated and

---

3. The meaning which the words "reality" and "realism" have acquired for many of our contemporaries is highly significant; "reality" has become synonymous with banality and even triviality, and thus with ugliness and brutality; in such a "realism" there is no longer room for truth, nobility or beauty, for values, that is, which elude quantitative measurement.

"instantaneous" character through which he rejoins, by a curious inverted analogy, the spiritual carefreeness of the man who is beyond caste *(ativarnāshramī)*, the *sannyāsī* who likewise lives in the "present moment," does not think of the morrow and wanders without apparent object; but the *shūdra* is too passive in relation to matter to be able to govern himself and therefore remains dependent on a will other than his own; his virtue is fidelity, or a kind of massive uprightness, no doubt opaque but simple and intelligible.

The qualities of *vaishyas* are often confused with those of *brāhmanas* and vice versa for the simple reason that both these castes are peaceable; and in the same way *shūdras* are apt to be confused with *kshatriyas* because of the aspects of violence proper to both castes; these errors are the more harmful inasmuch as we live in a civilization that is half *vaishya* and half *shūdra,* the values of which render such confusions easy. In such a world it is impossible to reach an understanding of the *brāhmana* without having first come to understand the values of the *kshatriya.* If facile confusions and unwarrantable assimilations are to be avoided, it is essential to differentiate sharply and on every plane between the higher and the lower, the conscious and the unconscious, the spiritual and the material, the qualitative and the quantitative.

It now remains for us to consider the case of the man who is "without caste"; here again it is a natural type, a basic human tendency, that we have in mind and not merely the categories that in fact occur in the Hindu system. We have seen that the typical *shūdra* can be opposed, because of his lack of real interest in what transcends his bodily life and the resulting lack of constructive aptitudes, to the three higher castes taken together; in a similar way the "outcast," by reason of his chaotic character, can be opposed to all men of homogeneous character. The "untouchable" exhibits a tendency to realize those psychological possibilities which are excluded for others: hence his proneness to transgression; he finds his satisfaction in what others reject. According to the Hindu the extreme type of the casteless man — the *chandāla* properly so called — is the offspring of a *shūdra* father and a *brāhmanī* mother; here the basic idea is that the maximum of impurity — or in other words of psychological dissonance due to congenital incompatibilities — arises from a maximum difference between the castes of the parents; the child of *shūdra* parents is "pure," thanks to their mental homogeneity, but the child born of the mixture of a *shūdra* and a noble woman is "impure" to the very degree of the superiority of the woman's caste over that of her husband. In Christian countries, as almost everywhere else, an illegitimate child, the "fruit of sin," is in practice regarded as "impure"; from the Hindu standpoint, which is centered in a kind of organic purity, this initial sin is hereditary in the same way as to be noble-born in Europe, or as "original sin" is in the Christian perspective.[4] All things considered the pariah, whatever his ethnic

---

4. "Illicit mingling of castes, marriages contrary to the rules and the omission of prescribed rites are the origin of the impure classes," says the *Mānava Dharma Shāstra* (X. 24). According to Shri Ramakrishna "the rules of caste are automatically effaced for the man who has reached perfection and realized the unity of all things; but as long as this sublime experience has not been obtained no one can avoid feeling superiority towards some and inferiority towards others, and all ought to observe distinctions of caste. If a man in this state of ignorance feigns perfection by trampling on caste distinctions and living without restraint, he is certainly like an unripe fruit that has been made to ripen artificially. . . . Those who invoke the Name of God become saints. Krishna Kishore was a saintly man of Ariadaha. One day he went on a pilgrimage to Vrindavan. During his journey he became thirsty and, seeing a man near a well, asked him to draw a little water. The man excused himself, saying he was of a very low caste, being a cobbler and so unworthy to offer water to a brahmin. Krishna Kishore then said to him: "Purify yourself by pronouncing the Name of God! Say: Shiva! Shiva!" The man obeyed and then offered him water to drink and that orthodox brahmin drank it! How great was his faith! . . . Chaitanya and Nityananda used to transmit the

origin and cultural background, constitutes a definite type which normally dwells on the fringe of society and exhausts those possibilities which no one else is willing to touch. When he has talents — and one might say he is then capable "of anything and of nothing" — he often appears equivocal, unbalanced, sometimes simian, and protean if he is gifted; often he appears as a chimney-sweep, comedian or executioner, not to mention illicit occupations; in a word he shows a tendency either to follow bizarre or sinister activities; or simply to neglect established rules, in which he resembles certain saints, though of course by inverse analogy. So far as "impure" or "contemptible" trades are concerned it might be thought hypocritical to abandon to certain men activities one is not willing to pursue oneself though one has need of them, but it must not be forgotten that society has a right to protect itself against tendencies which could be harmful to it and to neutralize them by exercising them through the intermediacy of men who in a way embody them. As a "totality" society has "divine rights" which an individual as such — and inasmuch as he is a "part" — does not possess; in some cases the converse is also true. An individual may refrain from condemning; society is obliged to condemn.

Name of Hari (the initiation into ritual invocation, *japa yoga*) to everyone including pariahs and embraced them all. A brahmin without this love is no longer a brahmin; a pariah with this love is no longer a pariah. Through *bhakti* an untouchable becomes pure and is raised up" (*L'Enseignement de Ramakrishna,* published by J. Herbert). Here is an illustration of the particular virtue of *bhakti* with which we dealt in our *The Transcendent Unity of Religions.* If account be taken of the inevitable difference between the principle of caste and its social and historical crystallization, it will readily be understood that an individual brahmin may be intrinsically heretical — as were Dayananda Saraswati and Ram Mohan Roy — and that a pariah may be a saint through Knowledge, as was Tiruvalluvar, who is venerated by brahmins as an *avatāra* of Shiva; inferiority can arise within the framework of superiority and vice versa.

Even unvarying situations may, however, become attenuated with the passage of time: the casteless mass of India
benefits from the cosmic law of compensation through
having become quite numerous and because of the resulting collective homogeneity; number itself acts as an absor-
bent substance, for the mass as such has something of the
leveling innocence of earth; just as, according to Islamic
esoterism, the flames of hell will in the end become cold —
God being "essentially" and not "accidentally" good — so
the congenital transgression of the pariah, his "impurity,"
must become attenuated at the end of the age and even
completely reabsorbed in many cases, though without the
heredity of which the individual remains a link or part[5]
being on that account abolished. For these individuals the
fact of being a pariah is an aspect of *karma* — a consequence
of "former actions" — exactly as is a disease or any other
kind of misfortune for a member of a higher caste. On the
other hand this same exclusion — a bit like the condition
of widows — has a certain religious value for the pariahs
themselves, and this explains the refusal of most of them

---

5. According to the *Mānava Dharma Shāstra*, "a man who belongs to a
base class may be recognized by his actions. . . . The absence of noble
feelings, coarseness of speech, cruelty (malice) and a forgetfulness of
duties denote, here below, the man who owes his birth to a mother
deserving of contempt." These criteria can clearly no longer be directly
applied to the whole mass of the casteless any more than it can be said
that all members of higher castes possess the virtues appropriate to their
respective *dharmas*. It may be added that this aspect of the problem is
independent of the question of temple entry; even if it be admitted that
a certain social formalism may be suppressed by reason of new cyclic
conditions, which is incontestable, such an easing of external forms
would remain independent of any question of knowing whether pariahs
should have access to brahmin sanctuaries. A Hindu temple is something
very different from a church or a mosque; it is not a place of obligatory
worship but the dwelling place of a Divine Presence. The principle of
ritual exclusion, with the unquestionable dogmatic rights it implies, is
moreover known in all religions; one need only recall the Temple enclo-
sure at Jerusalem and the iconostasis of Orthodox Christian churches.

to escape from their condition by abandoning the Hindu world;[6] as a general rule such men are proud to belong to their particular pariah "caste," this being true even of *chandālas*.

Caste is the center of gravity of the individual soul; the extreme pariah type is without center and so lives on the periphery and in inversion; if he tends to transgression, that is because in a sense it lends him the center he lacks and thus in an illusory way frees him from his equivocal nature. His is a decentralized subjectivity, centrifugal and without recognized limits; he flees from the law, the norm, because that would bring him back to the center which by his very nature he avoids. The *shūdra* type is also "subjective," but this subjectivity is opaque and homogeneous and bound to the body which is an objective reality; the *shūdra* has the quality, and the defect, of being "solid." This can also be expressed as follows: the *brāhmana* is "objective" and centered in "spirit"; the *kshatriya* tends towards "spirit," but in a "subjective" way; the *vaishya* is "objective" on the plane of "matter"; the *shūdra* is "subjective" on that

6. The Shankaracharya of Kanchi has spoken of this as follows: "The caste system, while exercizing the role of a rigid discipline conducive to the general well-being of society, is neutralized in the case of highly developed personages such as Nandanar the pariah Saint, or Dharma Vyadha, or Vidura of the *Mahābhārata*. Nandanar, even in his state of spiritual ecstasy, refused to enter the precincts of the temple, but he felt himself transported by joy simply by seeing the sanctuary tower; and the Brahmin of the temple respected Nandanar as the Brahmin of Brahmins. . . . Diversity of *acharas*, including food, marriage, etc., has a purpose which in the end profits the whole of humanity. . . . The Shudra did sternly refuse to allow a Brahmana or a Kshattriya to live in his house and a Chandala would stubbornly resist a Brahmin's entrance into his quarters and, if a Brahmin happened to enter his locality even accidentally, the Chandalas of the locality would go through some purificatory ceremonies. This indicates that the responsibility for the preservation of the respective disciplinary *acharas* of any caste did not lie with the concerned caste alone but was a collective one that lay with every component part of the society at large" ("Our Spiritual Crisis," *The Hindu*, July 1956).

same plane. The first three castes — the "twice-born" of Hinduism — are therefore distinguished from the *shūdra* either by "spirit" or by "objectivity"; only the *shūdra* combines "matter" with "subjectivity." Like the *shūdra,* the *vaishya* is a materialist, but his is a materialism of wider interests; like the *brāhmana,* the *kshatriya* is an "idealist," but his "idealism" is more or less worldly or egocentric.

The lower caste not only lacks the mentality of the higher, but cannot even conceive of it exactly; besides, few things are more painful than psychological interpretations which attribute to the superior man intentions he could never possibly entertain. Such opinions merely reflect the small-mindedness of their authors, as can be observed *ad nauseam* in historical criticism or in the science of religions; men whose souls are fragmentary and opaque pretend that they can instruct us in the "psychology" of greatness and of the sacred.

*
* *

It was stated at the outset that the system of castes is based on the nature of things, that is to say on certain natural properties of humankind and of which it is a traditional application;[7] now, as always happens in such a case, the traditional system "creates" — or helps to create — those very factors of which it is itself an application. The Hindu system results from spiritual or intellectual differences and at the same time creates types that are all the more sharply differentiated; whether this is an advantage or a disadvantage or both at once, it is a fact and an unavoidable fact at that. In the same way, where there is a traditional absence of castes, the latter perspective not only derives from the real absence of differentiation between men but also actualizes it, that is to say, it eliminates in a certain sense those

---

7. Gandhi pointed out that "the caste system . . . is inherent in human nature, and Hinduism has simply made a science of it" (*Young India*).

factors which, in the opposite perspective, give rise to the system of castes. In Islam, where there is no priestly caste either in a hereditary or in a vocational sense, every man has in him something of the priest and none is wholly a layman or is even describable as "the common man." To take another example, it can be said that if every Moslem is "something of a priest," every Red Indian is "something of a prophet," at least in certain conditions and by reason of the particular structure of the Red Indian tradition which distributes the prophetic quality throughout the collectivity, though without thereby abolishing the prophetic function properly so called. If any one were minded to reproach Hinduism for having "created" the pariah, the West could just as well be reproached for "creating" sin, since here as elsewhere the concept contributes to realizing the thing itself by virtue of a concomitance that is inevitable in the case of any formal crystallization.

If Westerners have difficulty in understanding the caste system it is, however, chiefly because they underestimate the law of heredity, and this for the very simple reason that it has become more or less inoperative in an environment as chaotic as the modern West where almost everyone aspires to climb the social ladder — if indeed such a ladder can still be said to exist — and where hardly anyone follows his father's calling. A century of two of such conditions have been enough to render heredity highly precarious and unstable, and all the more so since heredity was not in the past turned to account by a system as strict as that of the Hindu castes; but even where crafts transmitted from father to son did exist, machines have practically abolished heredity. To this must be added, on the one hand, the virtual elimination of the nobility and, on the other, the creation of new "elites"; the most disparate and "opaque" elements have been turned into "intellectuals" with the result that, as Guénon would have said, hardly anyone is any longer "in his proper place"; nor is there anything surprising in the fact that "metaphysical knowledge" has now come to be envisaged in accordance with the perspective of *vaishyas* and *shūdras,* a change which no amount of clap-trap about "culture" can conceal.

The problem of castes leads us to open a parenthesis here: how is the position or quality of the modern industrial worker to be defined? In the first place the answer is that "the worker's world" is a wholly artificial creation due to machines and the popular diffusion of scientific information connected with their use; in other words machines infallibly create the artificial human type called "proletarian," or rather they create a proletariat, for here it is essentially a question of a quantitative collectivity and not of a natural caste, namely one that is based on a particular individual nature. If machines could be suppressed and the ancient crafts restored with all their aspects of art and dignity, the "problem of the workers" would cease to exist; this is true even as regards purely servile functions or more or less quantitative occupations, for the simple reason that machines are in themselves inhuman and anti-spiritual. The machine kills not only the soul of the worker, but the soul as such and so also the soul of the exploiter: the pair exploiter-worker is inseparable from mechanization, whereas the crafts by their human and spiritual quality prevent this gross alternative. The universe of the machine means, in short, the triumph of ponderous and treacherous iron-mongery; it is the victory of metal over wood, of matter over man, of cunning over intelligence;[8] expressions such as "mass," "block" and "shock" that occur so commonly in the vocabulary of industrialized man, are very significant in a world more proper to insects than to humans. There is nothing surprising in the fact that the "workers' world," with its mechanico-scientific and materialistic psychology, is

---

8. Somewhere we have read that only the advances in technology can explain the new and catastrophic character of the first world war, and this is very true. Here it is machines that have made history, just as moreover they are making men, ideas and an entire world.

particularly impermeable to spiritual realities, for it presupposes a "surrounding reality" which is quite artificial: it requires machinery and therefore metal, din, hidden and treacherous forces, a nightmare environment, incomprehensible comings and goings, in a word an insect-like existence carried on in the midst of ugliness and triviality. In such a world, or rather in such a "stage set," spiritual reality comes to be regarded as an all too obvious illusion or a luxury to be despised. In no matter what traditional environment, on the contrary, it is the "problem of the workers," and so also of mechanization, which is devoid of persuasive force: in order to make it convincing, a world of stage sets corresponding to it had first to be created, in which the very forms suggest the absence of God; Heaven has to be implausible and talk of God has to sound false.[9] When the industrial worker says he has no time to pray he is not so wrong, for in this way he is merely expressing what is inhuman or, one might say, subhuman in his condition. The ancient crafts were eminently intelligible and did not deprive man of his human quality, which by definition implies the faculty to think of God. Some will doubtless object that industrialism is a fact and must be accepted as such, as though the character of being a fact took precedence over truth. People easily mistake for courage and realism what is their exact opposite: that is to say, because some calamity cannot be prevented, people call it a "good"

9. The great mistake of those who in Europe seek to lead the industrial masses back to the fold of the Church is that they confirm the worker in his "dehumanization" by accepting the world of machines as a real and legitimate world and even believing themselves obliged to "love that world for its own sake." To translate the Gospels into slang or to travesty the Holy Family in the guise of proletarians is to make a mockery not only of religion but of the workers themselves; it is in any case base demagogy or, let us say, weakmindedness, for all these attempts betray the inferiority complex of "intellectuals" when they meet the sort of "brutal realism" characteristic of the industrial worker. This "realism" becomes the more easy the more its field is limited, gross and so also unreal.

and make a virtue of their own inability to escape from it. Error is deemed truth simply because it exists and this fits in well with the dynamism and existentialism of the mentality of a machine age; everything that exists, thanks to the blindness of men, is called "our time," just as if this fact by itself constituted a categorical imperative. It is all too clear that the impossibility of escaping from an ill does not prevent that ill from being what it is; in order to find a remedy it is necessary to consider the ill quite apart from our chance of escape or our desire not to perceive it, for no good can arise in opposition to truth.

There is a common mistake, and one characteristic of the positivist or existentialist mentality of our times, which consists in believing that the establishing of a fact depends on knowing its causes or the remedies for it as the case may be, as if man had not a right to see things he can neither explain nor modify; to point out an evil is called "barren criticism" and one forgets that the first step towards a possible cure is to establish the nature of the disease. In any case, every situation offers the possibility, if not of an objective solution, at least of a subjective evaluation, a liberation by the spirit; whoever understands the real nature of machinery will at the same time escape from psychological enslavement to machines, and this is already a great gain. We say this without any optimism and without losing sight of the fact that the present world is a necessary evil whose metaphysical root lies in the last analysis in the infinity of Divine Possibility.

There is yet another objection to be reckoned with: some will say there have always been machines and those of the nineteenth century are merely more perfect, but this argument contains a radical error that one encounters again and again in varying forms; it arises from a lack of any feeling for "dimensions" or, to put it in another way, from an inability to distinguish between qualitative and "eminent" differences and those which are quantitative or accidental. The old looms, for example, even when highly perfected, are a kind of revelation and a symbol which by its intelligibility allows the soul to breathe, whereas a mechanized loom is suffocating for the man who serves it; the genesis of the craft of weaving goes hand in hand with spiritual life — as also appears from its aesthetic quality — whereas a modern machine on the contrary presupposes a mental climate and a labor of research incompatible with sanctity, not to speak of its resemblance to some giant arthropod or to a magic box, a fact which also counts as a criterion. A saint might construct or perfect a windmill or a water mill, but no saint could invent a machine, precisely because technical progress of this kind implies a mentality contrary to spirituality, and this criterion is evinced with brutal clarity, as has just been said, in the very forms of mechanical constructions.[10]

It must be emphasized that in the realm of forms, as in that of the spirit, everything is false which is not consonant either with virgin nature or with a sanctuary; everything legitimate is connected with nature on the one hand and with the sacred on the other. One striking characteristic of machines is that they feed insatiably on materials, these being often of a tellurian and darksome character, instead of being set in motion by man alone or by some natural force such as wind or water; in order to keep them "alive" man is forced to resort to a wholesale pillaging of the earth, and this is not the least aspect of their function of disequilibrium. A man must be blind indeed not to see that neither speed nor overproduction is a benefit, not to mention the reducing of the people to a

---

10. Attempts which, in antiquity and in the Middle Ages, came nearest to mechanical inventions were those that served chiefly for amusement and were regarded as curiosities and thus as things which became legitimate by very reason of their exceptional character. The ancients were not like feckless children who handle anything within reach, but on the contrary like men of ripe judgment who avoid certain orders of possibilities whose disastrous consequences they foresee.

proletariat and the disfigurement of the world.[11] But the basic argument remains the one first mentioned: such technology can only be born in a world without God, a world in which cunning has taken the place of intelligence and contemplation.

*

*   *

After this digression let us return to our fundamental theme: it is easy for a Westerner to understand how the equality of men before God springs from the very nature of things, and all the more so since the monotheistic religions — as well as Buddhism — by their very structure neutralize the inconveniences which can result from human inequalities; the fact that they accept these on the lay or worldly plane and on the other hand also create religious hierarchies, in no way impairs their fundamental perspective. Some may ask themselves why, granted that such a "leveling" is spiritually possible, Hinduism could not adopt the same point of view and abandon caste; now Hinduism as such, in other words as a totality, has neither the right nor the power to do this, since it goes without saying that, if a sacred institution exists, that is because it is metaphysically possible and therefore necessary, and this implies that it offers advantages which could not be realized otherwise.[12]

11. We can well guess that some would refuse us the moral right to make use of modern inventions, as if the economic structure and rhythms of our period would allow one to escape from these inventions or as if it were useful for one man to escape when no one else is able to do so. This refusal would moreover be logical only if all those values which the modern world has destroyed were restored to us.

12. Moreover the caste system proves its legitimacy by its results: "We do not think" wrote a missionary on the subject of the brahmins, "that there exists in the world an aristocratic family or even a royal family which has defended itself so pitilessly against every contagion, every missalli-

In fact, the pure and direct character of Vedantic metaphysics would be inconceivable apart from the caste system; in India the most transcendent intellectuality enjoys complete liberty, whereas in other traditions this same intellectuality has to accommodate itself to an esoterism more or less sybilline or even "tortuous" in its formulations and often also to certain sentimental restraints; this is the price paid for simplification of the social order. In the Semitic religions esoterism is closely bound up with exoterism and vice versa; the absence of castes imposes a certain mental uniformity which, from the point of view of pure metaphysics offers disadvantages not less than those the caste system offers from the point of view of the imponderables of human nature; exoterism is very apt to trespass on esoterism and this leads to an oscillation between these two planes to which a man like Omar Khayyam, an orthodox Sufi, replied by paradox and irony.[13] Where there exists a sharply defined exoterism, esoterism can hardly avoid "walking on exoteric stilts," although in reality it represents the essence of truth which transcends and incidentally shatters forms, as is shown by a case like that of Al-Hallaj, a lover of God whom the Hindus would assuredly not have condemned. It

ance, every physical or moral taint. That is why, personally speaking, we cannot conceal the fact that our contact with this splendid caste has left us truly dazzled and, from the bottom of our heart, profoundly sympathetic. . . . To the prestige of plastic beauty the brahmin visibly unites that of intelligence. Especially is he gifted to an extraordinary extent for the abstract sciences, for philosophy, and above all for mathematics. A man who on this score is certainly one of the most celebrated in South India, being a member of the higher council of professors of the Madras University, the Rev. Father Honoré, declared to us that the average level of the countless brahmin pupils he had taught during half a century as a teacher was far above, not only the average, but even the highest category of students in European universities" (Pierre Lhande: *L'Inde Sacrée*). "There is no doubt that caste (sub-castes of *vaishyas* and *shūdras* are meant here) offers many advantages to its members. It makes their work as easy, agreeable and honorable as possible; it excludes competitions properly so called, distributes a given quantity of work among the largest

130

must not be forgotten that the collectivity represents a principle of tending to increase density and complexity; it is always ready to lend an absolute character to facts, and this is the tendency of which religious dogmatism takes account from the outset. If esoterism can infuse into the mass something of its mysteries and graces, the mass in return lends it — to the extent that esoterism opens itself to the mass — its own tendencies to both "density" and "dissipation," whence a doctrinal simplification and a need for external activities which are the very antipodes of intellection and contemplation. For example, in Islam four levels must be distinguished: first there is exoterism as such (*sharī'ah*), which includes the ideas and means proper to its nature; then there is esoterism (*ḥaqīqah* or *taṣawwuf*) within exoterism, comprising whatever exoterism has been able or even compelled to assimilate of the former, the division between the two levels not being absolute; but such assimilation always remains a personal and mystical matter and in no way affects the sacred law. Then there is the inverse situation in which the exoteric perspective infiltrates into esoterism through a partial popularization that is historically inevitable; this is a perspective of activity and of merit,

---

possible number of available persons, looks after them in case of unemployment and defends their interests by the most varied means. . . . On the other hand, the fact that a profession is transmitted from father to son in many respects guarantees the quality of the work; through his heredity a man reaches an almost organic qualification for a particular activity which would be difficult to realize in any other way; at the same time technical secrets are handed on which enable craftsmen to produce masterpieces with most primitive means. Lastly the caste system has greatly contributed to the stabilization of Hindu society and the preservation of its civilization . . ." (H. von Glasenapp: *Der Hinduismus*).

13. If religious hypocrisy is an inevitable fact, the contrary must also be possible, and moreover hypocrisy provokes it: namely wisdom and virtue hiding under appearances of scandal. Among the Moslem *malāmatiyah* (the "people of blame") an attitude of this kind even forms part of their method.

of fear and of zeal combined with esoteric ideas;[14] finally there is an "esoterism within esoterism," if such an expression is possible, which is nothing other than gnosis disengaged, not indeed from all form, but from all inward formalism and all mythological absolutism.

As for the positive aspects of Moslem "leveling," Islam not only neutralized differences of caste, it also abolished racial oppositions. Perhaps no other civilization has mingled races so much as the Islamic one: in general the mulatto appears in Islam as a perfectly "pure" and honorable element, not as the pariah he is in practice among peoples of Christian origin; it could be said that for the Moslem the turban or fez is what a white skin is for a European. For Islam the determinations of nature are accidents; slavery is an accident and therefore has no relation to any caste system; humanity was originally without castes and without races; this is what Islam wishes to restore in conformity with the conditions of our millennium.[15] In Christianity and Buddhism the situation is similar: any man of sound mind can become a priest or monk; the clergy correspond to a vocational caste, not a hereditary one like the nobility, but the absence of a hereditary character is compensated by celibacy. We have already hinted at the fact

14. It cannot be denied, for instance, that the Sufism of Al-Ghazali includes a popular aspect which, though providential in its way, necessitates new inward adjustments.

15. The Prophet, after his victorious entry into Mecca, made many declarations, one of which is the following: "God has removed from you the pride of paganism and pride of ancestry; you all descend from Adam and Adam was dust. God said: 'Oh men, We have created you from a single man and a single woman, and We have divided you into peoples and tribes in order that you might know yourselves; he is the most honored of God who fears God the most.' " The Caliph Ali expressed it thus: "Nobility is derived from high qualities and not from the mouldering bones of ancestors." What Islam aims at restoring is, to be more precise, the religion of Abraham, the primordial form of the Semitic current and thus an image of the primordial tradition in its absolute sense, the tradition of the "Golden Age."

that, on condition of celibacy, Hinduism would admit that in principle a non-brahmin could become a brahmin by virtue of his individual aptitude and his vocation, for the risk of negative atavisms would then be eliminated; something of the kind does in fact exist in the state of the *ativarnāshramī*, who is beyond the castes but only on the condition of withdrawing his person from the living body of society. The fact that there are orders of *sannyāsīs* which admit only brahmins in no wise hinders any man from becoming a *sannyāsī* outside these orders. It should also be noted that three of the *avatāras* of Vishnu, namely Rama, Krishna and the Buddha, were *kshatriyas* and not *brāhmanas*, though clearly they must have possessed the brahminical nature in the highest degree; here can be seen a manifestation of universality as well as a compensation, for God, in His direct and flashing manifestations, does not submit to pre-existing frameworks, a derogation demanded by His infinitude.

To forestall any misinterpretation, it is important to note here that the absence of proper castes in Islam, and even in most non-Hindu traditions, has nothing to do with a "humanitarian" attitude in the current sense, and this for the simple reason that the point of view of tradition is that of the global interest of human beings, not just of what is pleasant; it has no use for a pseudo-charity that saves bodies but kills souls.[16] Tradition is centered on what gives meaning to life, not on an immediate "welfare" that is partial and ephemeral and conceived as an end in itself; it does not

16. The Gospels say: "Fear not them which kill the body but are not able to kill the soul" and, again, "What shall it profit a man if he shall gain the whole world and lose his own soul?" We certainly have no wish to criticize genuine charity such as springs from a total and not from a fragmentary vision of man and of the world. What is culpable is the exaggerated and specifically modern humanitarianism founded on the error that "the totality of all living beings is the Personal God . . . If only I can adore and serve the only God that exists, the sum total of all souls"

deny the relative and conditional legitimacy of such welfare but subordinates all values to the final ends of man. Unfortunately spiritual welfare is for most men not compatible with an earthly welfare that is too absolute; human nature has need of trials as well as consolations. A particular individual, whether rich or poor, may be sober and detached by his own will, but a collectivity is not an individual nor is it endowed with a single will; it always has something of the nature of an avalanche held in check and it maintains its balance only with the help of constraints, and indeed the hereditary virtues which strike us in some particular ethnic group are preserved only thanks to a continual struggle, whatever the plane on which this is carried out; this struggle itself forms part of happiness provided it remains close to nature, which is maternal, and does not become abstract and treacherous.

On the other hand it must not be forgotten that "welfare" is by definition something relative; once an exclusively material point of view is adopted the normal balance between spirit and body is destroyed and appetites are unleashed which carry with them no limiting factor. It is this aspect of human nature which humanitarians, in the usual sense of the term, either deny or deliberately ignore; they believe in man as good in himself, thus apart from God, and they arbitrarily ascribe his defects to unfavorable material conditions, as if experience did not prove not only that human malice does not depend on any outward factor, but also that it often develops in the midst of well-being, and sheltered from all elementary cares; the deviations of "bourgeois culture" exemplify this to repletion. For the

(Vivekananda). This philosophy is doubly false, first, because it denies God by decisively altering the notion of the Divine and, secondly, because it deifies the world and thus restricts charity to the most external level; one cannot see God in one's neighbor if one reduces a priori the Divine to the human. Nothing then remains but the illusion of "doing good," of being indispensable, and the contempt for those who "do nothing" even if they are saints whose presence sustains the world.

religions the "economic norm" is expressly the state of poverty, in which the Founders have always set the example — a poverty that stays close to nature, not of a denudation rendered unintelligible and ugly by the servitudes of an artificial and irreligious world; as for riches, they are tolerated because they are a natural right and exclude neither detachment nor sobriety — but they are never regarded as an ideal as is practically speaking the case in the modern world.

In this respect Hinduism is particularly strict: according to the *Shāstras* luxury properly so called — which envisages only physical well-being and keeps adding to it fresh needs — is a "theft from nature"; its opposite, simplicity, clearly means, not a privation of what is necessary, but a refusal of whatever is superfluous from the point of view of physical comfort, not a rejection of property as such; it is true that this stage of simplicity has been transcended in India itself, as elsewhere, and has been so for many centuries. Be that as it may, people today far too readily include under the common denomination of "misery" both an ancestral simplicity of life and mere lack of food, a confusion that is far from unbiased; the catchword "underdeveloped countries" is from this point of view highly significant in its candid perfidy. A scientific machine-age "standard of living" has been invented and the aim is to impose this on all peoples,[17] above all on those who are classed as "backward" whether they be Hindus or Hottentots. For these believers in progress happiness means a host of noisy and ponderous complications calculated to crush out many elements of beauty and hence of well-being; in wishing to

---

17. The Shankaracharya of Kanchi has pointed out in the text already quoted that "the very idea of raising the standard of living . . . will have the most injurious effects on society. Raising the standard of living means tempting people to encumber themselves with more luxuries and thus leading them ultimately to real poverty in spite of increased production. *Aparigraha* meant that every man should take from nature only so much as is required for his life in this world."

abolish particular "fanaticisms" and "horrors" these people forget that there are also atrocities on the spiritual plane and that the so-called humanitarian civilization of the moderns is saturated with them.

In order to be able to accurately judge the quality of happiness of an ancient world one would have to be able to put oneself in the place of the men who lived in it and adopt their way of evaluating things and so also their imaginative and sentimental reflexes; many things to which we have become accustomed would seem to them intolerable constraints to which they would prefer all the risks of their milieu; just the ugliness and the atmosphere of triviality of today's world would seem to them like the worst of nightmares. History as such cannot give a full account of the soul of some distant epoch: it chiefly registers calamities, leaving aside all the static factors of happiness; it has been said that happiness has no history, and this is profoundly true. Wars and epidemics — no more than certain customs — clearly do not reflect the happy aspects of the lives of our ancestors, while their literary and artistic works do so. Even if one supposes that history could tell us nothing about the happiness of the Middle Ages, the cathedrals and other artistic manifestations of the medieval world provide an indisputable witness in that sense, which is to say they do not give the impression of a humanity more unhappy than that of today to say the least; like the Orientals of old the ancestors of the present Europeans would no doubt have preferred, given the choice, to be unhappy after their own fashion than happy after ours. There is nothing human which is not an evil from some point of view: even tradition itself is in certain respects an "evil," since it must handle evil things in man and these human ills invade it in their turn, but it is then a lesser evil, or a "necessary evil," and, humanly speaking, it would obviously be far truer to call it a "good." The pure truth is that "God alone is good" and that every earthly thing has some ambiguous side to it.

No doubt some will say that humanitarianism, far from being materialistic by definition, aims at reforming human nature by education and legislation; now it is contradictory to want to reform the human outside the divine since the latter is the essence of the former; to make the attempt is in the end to bring about miseries far worse than those from which one was trying to escape. Philosophical humanitarianism underestimates the immortal soul by the very fact that it overestimates the human animal; it is somewhat obliged to denigrate saints in order to better whitewash criminals; the one seems unable to go without the other. From this results oppression of the contemplatives from their most tender years: in the name of humanitarian egalitarianism, vocations are crushed and geniuses wasted, by schools in particular and by official worldliness in general; every spiritual element is banished from professional and public life[18] and this amounts to removing from life a great part of its content and condemning religion to a slow death. The modern leveling — which may call itself "democratic" — is the very antipodes of the theocratic equality of the monotheistic religions, for it is founded, not on the theomorphism of man, but on his animality and his rebellion.

The thesis of indefinite progress moreover comes up against the following contradiction: if man has been able to exist for thousands of years under the domination of errors and stupidities — supposing that the traditions are merely such, in which case the error and stupidity would be well-nigh measureless — the immensity of this deception would be incompatible with the intelligence with which man as such is credited and with which he must be credited. In

---

18. On the other hand, by a kind of compensation, professional life more and more assumes a "religious" air in the sense that it claims the whole of man, his soul as well as his time, as though the sufficient reason for the human condition were some economic enterprise and not immortality.

other words, if man is intelligent enough to arrive at the "progress" which our period embodies — assuming there is any reality in such progress — then man must have been a priori too intelligent to remain for thousands of years the dupe of errors as ridiculous as those which modern "progressivism" attributes to him; and if he is on the contrary stupid enough to have believed in them so long, then he must also be too stupid to escape from them. Or again, if present day man had at long last arrived at truth, he would have to be proportionately superior to the men of former times, and the disproportion between the two would be almost absolute. Now the least that can be said is that the men of ancient or medieval times were neither less intelligent nor less virtuous that modern man, far from it. The ideology of progress is one of those absurdities that are as remarkable for the lack of imagination as for the total lack of sense of proportion they display; this is, moreover, essentially a *vaishya* illusion, rather like that of "culture," which is nothing more than an intellectuality stripped of intelligence.

*

* *

To return now to the question of castes: the absence of outward castes — for natural castes can be annulled only in sanctity, at least in certain respects — this absence requires conditions which neutralize the possible disadvantages of such a social indifferentiation; in particular it requires a code of behavior safeguarding the spiritual liberty of every man; by this is meant, not liberty for error, which obviously has no spiritual character, but liberty for a life in God. Such a code of behavior is the very negation of an egalitarian leveling, for it concerns what is highest in us: men are enjoined to dignity and should treat one another as potential saints; to bow to one's neighbor is to see God everywhere and to open oneself to God. The opposite attitude is the "camaraderie" which denies one's neighbor all mystery and even any right to mystery; it means putting oneself on the level of human animality and reducing one's neighbor to that same level, forcing him into a stifling and subhuman flatness. An absence of social differences can only exist on a religious basis: it can be brought about only from above, first by attaching man to God and then by recognizing the presence of God in man. In a civilization such as Islam there are, strictly speaking, no "social milieus" properly so called; the rules of good conduct form part of religion and it is enough to be pious in order to know them; a poor man therefore feels at ease among the rich, the more so in that religion is "on his side" since poverty, viewed as a state, is a perfection; nor is a rich man shocked by any lack of education or "culture" among the poor, for there is no "culture" apart from the tradition whose point of view moreover is never quantitative. In other words, the poor man can be an "aristocrat" beneath his rags, whereas in the West it is "civilization" itself which prevents this. It is true that one may meet peasant aristocrats even in present-day Europe, especially in the Mediterranean countries, but they give the impression of being survivals from another age; the modern leveling everywhere destroys the beauties of religious equality, for the former being the caricature of the latter, they are incompatible.

Caste, as we mean it, has in essence two aspects, one of "degree" and the other of "mode" of intelligence, a distinction due, not to the essence of the intellect, but to accidents of its manifestation. Intelligence may be contemplative or inquiring, intuitive or discursive, direct or indirect; it may be simply inventive or constructive; or it may amount to no more than elementary common sense; in each of these modes there are degrees so that one man may be more "intelligent" than another while remaining inferior to him from the point of view of mode. In other words intelligence may be centered on the intellect, which is transcendent and infallible in its essence, or on reason, which has no direct perception of transcendent realities and consequently cannot provide a guarantee against a passionate element intruding into thought; reason may be to a greater or lesser extent determined by the intellect, but it may also be limited to things of practical life or even to life's most immediate and rudimentary aspects. Now, as has already been explained, the caste system derives essentially from a perspective of intelligence and so of intellectuality and metaphysical knowledge, hence the spirit of exclusiveness and purity so characteristic of the Hindu tradition.

The equality, or rather the indifferentiation, realized by Buddhism, Islam and other traditions is related to the pole of "existence" rather than to that of "intelligence"; existence, the being of things, neutralizes and unites, whereas intelligence discerns and separates. Existence by its very nature is an "exit" (*ex-sistere, ex-stare*) out of Unity and thus is the plane of separation, whereas intelligence, being Unity by its intrinsic nature, is the ray leading back to the Principle. Both existence and intelligence unite and divide, but each does so in a different relationship, so that intelligence divides where existence unites and vice versa. This could be put in another way: for Buddhism — which does not expressly deny the castes but rather ignores them — all men are "one," first of all in suffering and then in the Path to Deliverance; for Christianity all are "one," first through original sin and then in baptism, the pledge of Redemption; for Islam all are "one," first because they are created from dust and then in unitary faith; but for Hinduism, which starts from Knowledge and not from man, it is above all Knowledge which is "one" while men are diverse by the degree of their participation in Knowledge and so also by the degree of their ignorance; it might be said that they are "one" in Knowledge, but Knowledge in its intrinsic purity is not accessible save to an elite, whence the exclusiveness of the *Brāhmins*.

The individual expression of intelligence is discernment; the individual expression of existence is the will. As we have seen, the perspective which gives rise to castes is based on man's intellectual aspect; man, for this perspective, is intelligence, discernment; on the other hand, the perspective of social indifferentiation, which relates to the pole "existence," starts from the idea that man is will and distinguishes between two tendencies in the will, the one spiritual and the other worldly, just as the perspective of intellect and caste distinguishes between different degrees of intelligence or ignorance. In this way it can be understood why *bhakti* practically speaking ignores caste and may allow initiation even of pariahs[19]: it is because *bhakti* sees in man a priori will and love and not intelligence and intellection; consequently there is, side by side with the castes based on "knowing," another hierarchy based on "willing," so that human categories cross one another like the threads in a weaving; spiritual "willing" is, however, met with far more often where there is a "knowing."

*
* *

Psychologically speaking a natural caste is a cosmos; men live in different cosmoses according to the "reality" on which they are centered; it is impossible for the inferior really to understand the superior, for he who really understands "is" what he understands. On the other hand it can be said that all these human categories are found again in some way, even if it be in a quite indirect or wholly symbolical manner, not only within each of the aforementioned categories but also in every man. There is likewise a certain analogy between castes and ages in the sense that the lower types are found in certain aspects of childhood while the passionate and active type is represented by the adult and the contemplative and serene type by the aged; it is true that in the case of a coarse man the process is often reversed, for he retains, after outgrowing the illusions of youth, only his materialism, and he identifies with those

---

19. There are doubtless also such exceptions in *jñāna*.

illusions what little of nobility youth had once lent him. But we must not forget that each of these fundamental types has virtues which characterize it, so that the non-brahminical types have a significance that is not merely privative; the *kshatriya* has nobility and energy, the *vaishya* honesty and practical cleverness, the *shūdra* fidelity and diligence; the contemplativity and detachment of the brahmanical type contain all these qualities in an eminent degree.

The principle of caste is reflected, not only in the ages of man, but also in a different way in the sexes: woman is opposable to man, in a sense, as the chivalrous type is opposable to the sacerdotal, or again, in another relationship, as the "practical" type is opposable to the "idealist," one might say. But, just as the individual is not absolutely bound by caste, neither can he be bound in an absolute way by sex: the metaphysical, cosmological, psychological and physiological subordination of woman is apparent enough, but woman is nonetheless the equal of man from the point of view of the human condition and so also of immortality; she is his equal in respect of sanctity, but not in respect of spiritual functions; no man can be more holy than the Blessed Virgin, and yet, any priest can celebrate the Mass and preach in public, whereas she could not. From another angle woman assumes, with regard to man, an aspect of Divinity: her nobility, compounded of beauty and of virtue, is for man like a revelation of his own infinite essence thus of what he "wishes to be" because that is what he "is."

Finally we would like to touch on a certain connection between the actualization of castes and sedentarism: it is an undeniable fact that the lower types are less frequently found among warrior nomads than among sedentary peoples; adventurous and heroic nomadism results in the qualitative differences becoming as it were submerged in a generalized nobility; the materialistic and servile type is kept in abeyance and in compensation the priestly type does not become completely distinct from the chivalric type. According to the conception of these peoples, human quality — nobility — is maintained by a fighting mode of life: no virtue, they say, without virile and therefore perilous activity; man becomes vile when he ceases to look suffering and death in the face; it is impassiveness which makes a man: it is the event, or, adventure one could say, that makes life. This perspective explains the attachment of these peoples — Bedouins, Tuaregs, Red Indians and ancient Mongols — to their ancestral nomadic or semi-nomadic condition and the contempt they feel for sedentary folk and especially for town-dwellers; the deepest evils from which humanity is suffering do in fact come out of the great urban agglomerations and not from virgin nature.[20]

*

* *

In the cosmos all things present at the same time an aspect of simplicity and an aspect of complexity, and in every sphere there are perspectives related to either the one or the other of these aspects; synthesis and analysis alike are in the nature of things, and this is true of human societies as of other orders; it is therefore impossible that castes be found nowhere, or that they nowhere be absent. Strictly speaking Hinduism has no "dogmas," in the sense that in it every concept may be denied provided the argument is intrinsically true; but this absence of "irremovable" dogmas in the strict sense at the same stroke prevents social unification. What makes such unification possible, in particular in the monotheistic religions, is precisely dogma which serves as a transcendent Knowledge accessible to all. If to the majority of men Knowledge as such is inaccessible, it yet imposes itself on all in the form of faith, so that the

20. A certain easing of the Hindu system among the Balinese can be explained by facts qualitatively analogous to nomadism, namely their insular isolation and the necessarily restricted number of the inhabitants; also the Balinese show a proud and independent character which makes them akin to the nomads.

believer is something like a virtual or symbolical *brāhmana.*
The exclusiveness of the *brāhmana* in regard to the other
castes is repeated, *mutatis mutandis,* in the exclusiveness of
the believer in regard to unbelievers or to the "unfaithful";
in both cases it is "Knowledge" which excludes, whether it
be a matter of hereditary aptitude for pure Knowledge or
the fact of a symbolical and virtual knowledge, that is to say
a religious belief. But both in the case of a revealed faith
and in that of an instituted caste, the exclusion — conditional and "offensive" in the former case and unconditional and "defensive" in the latter — may be only
"formal" and not "essential," for every saint is a "believer"
whatever his religion and a *"brāhmin"* whatever his caste. It
should perhaps be made clear as regards dogmas that the
doctrinal pillars of Hinduism are in part "variable
dogmas"; which is to say that they lose their absolute quality
at higher levels while preserving it unshakably on the level
to which they relate, aside from all question of legitimate
divergences of perspective. But in all this no door is left
open to intrinsic error, for otherwise the tradition would
lose the very reason for its existence. Once we discern
between the true and the false, "heresy" becomes possible,
whatever may be our own reaction to it; it corresponds on
the level of ideas to material error on the level of facts.

In its spiritual sense, caste is the "law" or *dharma* governing a particular category of men in accord with their qualifications. It is in this sense, and only in this sense, that the
Bhagavad-Gītā says: "Better for each one is his own law of
action, even if imperfect, than the law of another, even well
applied. It is better to perish in one's own law; it is perilous
to follow the law of another" (III, 35).[21] And similarly the
Mānava-Dharma Shāstra says: "It is better to carry out one's

---

21. The *Bhagavad-Gītā* cannot mean that every individual must, when
he meets a traditional teaching, follow his personal opinions and tastes,
otherwise Hinduism, which is a tradition, would long ago have ceased to
exist.

own proper functions in a defective manner than to fulfill perfectly those of another; for he who lives accomplishing the duties of another caste forthwith loses his own" (X, 97).

The Meaning of Race

Caste takes precedence over race because spirit has priority over form; race is a form while caste is a spirit. Even Hindu castes, which were in origin purely Indo-European, cannot be limited to a single race: there are Tamil, Balinese and Siamese brahmins.[1] It is not possible, however, to hold that race is something devoid of meaning apart from physical characteristics, for, if it is true that formal constraints have nothing absolute about them, forms must nonetheless have their own sufficient reason; if races are not castes,[2] they must all the same correspond to human differences of another order, rather as differences of style may express equivalence in the spiritual order while also marking divergencies of mode.

Thus the thinking of a white man — whether a Westerner or an Easterner — is incisive and animated like his idioms and his facial features; one might say that there is something "auditory" about it, whereas the thinking of men of

1. The Siamese brahmins are a survival of Brahminism in the midst of a Buddhist civilization.
2. This is true at any rate of the major races, white, yellow and black, and of intermediary races such as the American Indians, the Malayo-Polynesians, the Dravidians and the dark-skinned Hamites; but it is always possible for quite small racial groupings to coincide broadly speaking with castes.

the yellow race has a more or less "visual" character[3] and works by discontinuous strokes. The spirit of the Far East may be called both static and aerial; its conciseness is compensated by its symbolical quality and its dryness by intuitive delicacy. The languages of white peoples, whether they be Hamito-Semitic or Aryan, are inflected and move in mental arabesques, productive of long, rich, incisive sentences. Those of yellow peoples, whether they be agglutinative or monosyllabic, disdain what we call "eloquence" and their mode of expression is sober and often elliptical; here beauty is lyrical rather than dramatic, for the yellow man lives in nature — in the visible and spatial — rather than in the human and temporal; his poetry is anchored in virgin nature and has no Promethean quality.[4]

The mental process of the yellow man is in a sense like his face, and, as was said above, the same is true of the white man and also of the black man. The black race bears in itself the substance of an "existential wisdom"; it asks for few symbols; it needs only a homogeneous system: God, prayer, sacrifice and dancing. Fundamentally the blacks have a "non-mental" mentality, whence the "mental" importance for them of what is corporal, their physical sureness and their sense of rhythm. In all these characteristics the black

3. Chinese writing, which is the most important script in the case of the yellow race and was conceived by them alone, is essentially "visual" and not "auditive"; it conveys pictures and not sounds.

4. Partisans of the short sentence want to treat our morphological languages like Chinese. Certainly the short sentence has a legitimate place in the languages of the white race, but their habitual mode of expression is by complex sentences: in Arabic a whole book is theoretically a single sentence. For the white man a sentence is a bundle of thoughts grouped around a central idea; for the yellow man, who is less exteriorized, it is a "suggestion," a "gong-stroke." Clearly those white peoples who speak Mongolian tongues — Finns, Magyars and Turks — use them differently than did their still Mongolian ancestors.

man may be contrasted both with the white man and with the yellow.[5]

The originality of each of the various races is especially apparent in the eyes: those of the white man, generally deep-set, are mobile, piercing and transparent; his soul "goes out" in his look and at the same time shines, in its passivity, through it. The eyes of yellow men are quite different: physically at skin level, they are generally indifferent and impenetrable; their look is dry and light like a brush-stroke on silk. As for the black man, his eyes are slightly prominent and heavy, warm and moist; their look reflects the beauty of the tropics and combines sensuality — sometimes ferocity — with innocence; it is the deep and latent look of the earth. The black man's eyes express what his face is, that is, a sort of heavy contemplativity, while in the case of the white man, who is more "mental," the face seems to express the living fire of his eyes; in the case of the yellow man the eyes pierce, like flashes of impersonal lucidity, through what is static or "existential" in the face. One of the chief charms of the Mongolian type is the complementary relationship between the existential passivity of the face — a certain "femininity" it might be said — and the implacable lucidity of the eyes, a cold and unexpected fire lighting up a mask.

In order to understand the meaning of races, one must first of all realize that they are derived from fundamental aspects of humanity and not from something fortuitous in nature. If racism is something to be rejected, so is an anti-racism which errs in the opposite direction by attributing racial difference to merely accidental causes and which seeks to reduce to nothing these differences by talking

---

5. We refer to the black race as such, which is independent of the degeneration of particular tribes. In general, it must not be forgotten that the present state of black Africa gives hardly any idea of those flourishing civilizations which impressed European and Arab travelers just after the close of the Middle Ages and which later were destroyed.

about inter-racial blood-groups, or in other words by mixing up things situated on different levels. Moreover, that the isolation of a race may have contributed to its elaboration certainly does not mean that this race can be explained in terms of its isolation alone, nor that the isolation was fortuitous and thus something which might not have happened. Again, the fact that there is nothing absolute in nature and that races are not separated in completely watertight compartments in no way means that pure races are not to be found as well as mixed ethnic groupings. Such an opinion has no meaning for the simple reason that all men have the same origin and that humanity as a whole — often wrongly referred to as the human race — constitutes one single species. Racial mixtures may be good or detrimental according to the case: mixing may "aerate" an ethnic stock that has become too "compact," just as it may bastardize a homogeneous group endowed with precise and precious qualities. What is never understood by those who have a passion for racial purity is that there is a greater qualitative difference between the psychic heredity of different natural castes — even if the race be the same — than between that of members of the same caste of different races; fundamental and personal tendencies have more importance than racial modes, at any rate insofar as the major races or their healthy branches are concerned, and not degenerate groups.[6]

Certain racial traits, which the white man tends to take for signs of inferiority, actually mark either a less mental —

6. A certain "segregation" of white and black people would be neither ill-judged nor unjust if it were not unilateral, that is to say, if it were conceived in the interest of both races and without prejudice of superiority; for it is clear that to abolish "segregation" altogether means increasing the probability of racial mixtures and vowing one's own race, whether it be white or black, to a kind of disappearance. In North Africa, where mixtures between black and white are more or less in the nature of things, as they have been for thousands of years, the problem is different: here the white people are as it were absorbed by the climate as well as by the

though not less spiritual — disposition than that of the average European or else a greater racial vitality. Here we must draw attention to the error of regarding prognathism, relatively low forehead or thick lips, as belonging to an obviously inferior type. If the white man looks on the yellow types as inferior to his own because they appear to him to share certain characteristics of the facial expression of the blacks, the yellow man could, with equal logic, see in the white and black types two divergent forms of degeneration between which his own type holds a right balance, and so on. As for the forehead, its height or cranial volume denotes — if it denotes anything, which depends on a variety of factors — by no means always an intellectual quality, but more often a capacity which is solely creative or even merely inventive, a capacity which may, by luciferian deviation, become a veritable hypertrophy of the mind — a specific propensity to "thinking," but not at all to "knowledge." No doubt the forehead should not be too low, but there is an adequate size suitable even to the most spiritual of men; if it is surpassed, that is in any case without any relation to pure intelligence.

Prognathism itself shows vital force and existential fullness, and thus a consciousness centered on "being," whereas the orthognathous type corresponds to a consciousness relatively detached from that pole, more or less "rootless" or "isolated" in relation to "being" and for that very reason "creative."[7] An orthognathous face is generally more "open" or more "personal" than one that is progna-

African quality of the surroundings so that mixtures have given birth to perfectly harmonious human groups; moreover in this case the white element is a Mediterranean one and not Germanic as in North America. Africans make a clear distinction between Mediterranean and Nordic white men, feeling themselves less far removed from the former than from the latter; it is also very probable that mixtures between human types as divergent as the Nordic and the Black are not very happy ones.

7. It should be noted that the faces of Bushmen and Melanesians are more or less orthognathous, while Malays and Indo-Chinese are often

thous; it exteriorizes its contents rather than its whole being, and this is as much as to say that it more readily shows what it feels and thinks; the nose is prominent as if to compensate for the retreating of mouth and eyes, all of which means a psychic tendency to "extroversion." This characteristic of the nose which often gives rise to the aquiline type — and the latter is met with in all races and always suggests analogous characteristics — indicates a cosmic connection with birds, and so with flight, with the skies and winds; there is an aspect of soaring and mobility, but also one of instability and fragility. The spirit of the white man — especially in the West where these features are generally more marked than in the East — has something of the quality of a restless and "devouring" fire; in its working it alternately "goes out" and "turns in on itself"; it "opens up" like fire, whereas the spirit of the yellow man is "closed in on itself" like water. The black man, for his part, seems an incarnation of the massiveness, at times volcanic, of the earth, whence comes the serene heaviness, or heavy serenity, that characterizes his beauty; his face can have the majesty of a mountain. Insofar as this both rough and sweet massiveness translates an aspect of Existence and can, for this reason, become the support for a contemplative attitude, it certainly is not a mark of inferiority. Let us add that the lugubrious side of Negro art and of animism in general as well as the sometimes rumbling, breathless and spasmodic tonality of African music are both connected with the ele-

markedly prognathous, and this shows the absurdity of the current view that a prognathous type goes with barbarism. If the fact that the peoples just mentioned are orthognathous does not give rise in their case to the same psychological consequences as it does in white peoples this is because it is neutralized by other racial factors, though without losing its significance: every form has meaning, but the meaning is not always actualized in the same way. It is not possible to interpret in a few lines the numerous combinations to which human types are liable, and moreover such is not our intention.

ment "earth," either in its cavernous, subterranean aspect or in its aspect of fertility and thus of sexuality.

The white race, whose thinking is more exteriorized, shows, when taken as a whole, a greater "disequilibrium" than the yellow or black races; within the yellow race there is perhaps no greater difference than that between the Mongols and the Malays, but this difference is less than that between Europeans and White Orientals; to go from France to Morocco is almost like traveling to another planet. The fact that a collectivity in general so little contemplative as the Europeans and another which is the most contemplative of all, the Hindus, can both belong to the same white race shows the essentially "differentiated" character of that race: a Tibetan would feel infinitely less "lost" in Japan — we mean ancient Japan — than a Hindu or an Arab in England — even in the England of the Middle Ages; but from another angle there is a profound mental difference between Hindus and Arabs. The radical diversity of religions among white peoples reflects their mental diversity, that character of theirs at once uneven and creative which, within the framework of European humanity, turns into disequilibrium and hypertrophy: the Mediterranean and Nordic races and then the pagan and Christian mentalities have never ceased throughout history to come into collision, for they have never been able to give birth to a sufficiently homogeneous humanity.

Here it is important to note that the religions created by the yellow race,[8] namely the tradition of Fo-Hi and the I-Ching, then Confucianism and Taoism connected with this, and finally Shintoism, did not give rise to fundamen-

---

8. This only in a manner of speaking, for it goes without saying that a religion is revealed by Heaven and not created by a race; but a revelation always conforms to a racial genius, although this by no means signifies that it is restricted to the specific limits of the race in question.

tally and irreducibly different civilizations as did the great religions of the white race: Christianity, Islam and Hinduism, not to mention the Greco-Roman West, Ancient Egypt and the other white civilizations of antiquity. Confucianism and Taoism are the two complementary branches issued from a single "prehistoric" tradition and share the same sacred language and the same ideograms; as for Shintoism, it does not concern all spiritual possibilities and so is not a total "religion" but requires a superior complement which Buddhism has provided, so that we find in Japan a traditional symbiosis such as is not to be found among white people; something similar could be said of Buddhism and Shamanism in Tibet and other countries. Be that as it may, what we want to underline here is that the difference between yellow-race civilizations is far less than that between West and East in the world of the white race;[9] to greater equilibrium, greater stability, there must correspond lesser differentiation.

The yellow and black people taken together are distinct from the whites in respect of their vitality and their lesser mental exteriorization, the yellow in a manner that is dry and light and the black in one that is heavy and humid; compared to these two races the white man is "hypersensitive." The yellow man, however, while being "static" like the black man has not the same "inertia," for he is both creative and industrious. What distinguishes the yellow man from both the white and the black is his intuitive delicacy, his artistic faculty of expressing imponderables, his passionlessness without inertia and his effortless equilib-

9. The only fundamental division in the Far East is that marking the separation of Northern Buddhism in Tibet, Mongolia, China, Manchuria, Annam, Korea and Japan, from Southern Buddhism in Burma, Siam, Cambodia and Laos; Northern Buddhism has been absorbed by the genius of the yellow race whereas in the South it is the racial genius that has been absorbed by Buddhism. Mahayana Buddhism is India become yellow, whereas the Theravadins of Indo-China are yellow people become Indians, as it were.

rium; he is more "dry," more impenetrable and less highly strung than the white man and "lighter," more agile and more creative than the black. Perhaps it might also be said that the white man is essentially a "poet"; his soul is at the same time animated and as it were "furrowed." The yellow man is first of all a "painter," an intuitive who visualizes things; his psychic life, as we have said, is more "smooth" and static and less "projected forwards" in the sense that things are viewed in the soul instead of the soul being projected into things. As for the black man, he is neither a "cerebral" nor a "visual" type but "vital," and so a born dancer; he is "profoundly vital" as the yellow man is "delicately visual," both races being existential rather than mental as compared to the white race. All these expressions can be no more than approximations, for everything is relative, especially in an order of things as complex as race. A race may be compared to a whole style of art with many forms rather than to one exclusive form.

The yellow type has this in common with the black that both are marked by a certain existential indifference — not by intellectual preoccupation, a "going out of oneself," by "research," or "penetration" — though in the yellow type this indifference is intuitive and lucid, not vegetative and passionate as in the case of the black type. We are almost tempted to say that the yellow man thinks in pictures, even abstract ones, rather than by speculations, while the black man thinks through "forces." The black man's wisdom is dynamic, it is a "metaphysic of forces." Note the very great importance among black peoples of tom-toms, the function of which is central and quasi-sacred: they are the vehicle for rhythms which, when communicated to human bodies, bring the whole being into contact with cosmic essences. However paradoxical it may seem, it is the intelligence rather than the body of the black man which is in need of rhythms and dances, and that precisely because his spirit has a plastic or existential and not an abstract way of approach;[10] the body, for the very reason that it is the limit of crystallization in the demiurgic process, represents "being" as opposed to "thought," or "our whole being" as opposed to our relatively particular preoccupations or to our outward consciousness. The roll of tom-toms marks, like heaven's thunder, the voice of Divinity: by its very nature and by its sacred origin it is a "remembrance of God," an "invocation" of the Power both creator and destroyer and thus also liberator, through which human art canalizes the divine manifestation and in which man participates through dancing; he thus participates with all his being in order to regain the heavenly fluidity through the "analogical vibrations" between matter and the Spirit. The drum is the altar, its roll marks the descent of God and the dance the ascent of man.[11]

10. To allow the black man to dance while subjecting him to a civilization in which dancing has no serious function is wholly inefficacious, for the black man can then use only "permitted dances" or "tolerated rites" or what is patronized as mere "folklore." He needs rhythms of bodies and of drums which he can take seriously, and this both Islam and Abyssinian Christianity offer him. We would readily believe that a particular black man, even in Africa, might not suffer consciously from not being able to dance to the sound of tom-toms; but this is not the question, for we speak of a collective integration and not of individual adaptation. In the case of the American blacks this need for bodily and musical rhythms has been maintained but can now be expressed only in trivial mode: that is the posthumous vengeance of a racial genius that has been trampled underfoot. In the same order of ideas, such a movement as the Mau-Mau is, in the final analysis, explained, not by "ingratitude" as some have stupidly asserted, but by the simple fact that black men are black men and not white men, to use a somewhat elliptical expression; and it is clear that something like this can be said of other similar cases. Let us add that there are no human beings devoid of all value; this is as much as to say that if men are allowed the right to exist they must also be allowed — in an effective way — the right to certain elements of their own culture.

11. We meet with the same symbolism in dervish dances and, in principle, in every ritual dance. Love dances, harvest dances, or war dances are designed to abolish the barriers between different levels of

To return now to the white race, we could, at the risk of repetition, characterize it by the terms "exteriorization" and "contrast"; what is exteriorized tends towards diversity and richness, but also towards a certain "creative rootlessness" which explains why the white race is alone in having given birth to a number of profoundly different civilizations, as has already been pointed out; further, the contrasts which among white people as a whole are produced "in space" and in simultaneity, have been produced in the case of Westerners "in time," during the course of European history. Let us add that, if the white man is a restless and devouring "fire," he can also be — as in the case of the Hindu — a calm and contemplative flame; as for the yellow man, if he is "water," he can reflect the moon but can also be unleashed in violent storms; if the black man is "earth," he has, besides the innocent massiveness of that element, the explosive force of volcanoes.[12]

Each of the three great races, and each of their great intermediate branches, produces perfect beauty, beauty incomparable and in a sense irreplaceable; it is necessarily thus because each of these types is an aspect of the human

existence and to establish a direct contact with the "genius" or "divine Name" in question. Human infidelities do not in any way change the principle or take away the value of the means: whatever may be the importance given to utilitarian considerations or to magical procedures in the case of some Negro animism or some Siberian or Red Indian shamanism, the symbols remain what they are and the bridges towards heaven are doubtless never altogether broken down.

12. These correspondences are founded on the visible elements, three in number. We do not know the source of the following classification: white race, water, lymphatic, north, winter; yellow race, air, nervous, east, spring; black race, fire, sanguine, south, summer; red race, earth, bilious, west, autumn. While this picture includes some plausible elements it calls for serious reservations. The fact that the red race includes a type not to be found anywhere else so precisely marked or so widespread does not authorize us to look on it as a fundamental race, for it also includes types that are found in the yellow and white races.

norm.[13] Compared to white beauty, yellow and black beauty seem much more sculptural; they are much nearer to substance and to femininity than the white type, a femininity which the black race expresses in tellurian mode and the yellow in celestial mode. At its peak yellow beauty realizes an almost immaterial nobility, often sweetened by a flower-like simplicity; white beauty is more personal and no doubt less mysterious because more explicit, though for that very reason very expressive and also marked at times by a kind of melancholy grandeur. It should perhaps be added that the Negroid type, at its finest, is not reducible merely to "earth"; it amounts rather to earth's precious concretions and thus escapes its primal heaviness: it then realizes a nobility like basalt, obsidian or jasper, a kind of mineral beauty which transcends the passional and evokes the immutable.

At the boundaries of the great races there is also a tropical type, more or less Negroid, passing like a weft through the white and yellow types in equatorial regions; this seems to indicate the important, though not exclusive, part played by climate in the elaboration of the black type. There is on the other hand no Nordic type found in the other races, so that it may be concluded that differentiation in the white and yellow races is due only to fundamental divergences of an inner order. However, broadly speaking, there is a Nordic temperament which is opposed to the tropical temperament: outside Europe and its ethnic dependencies the former is represented by the North American Indians — whose type is introvert and but little sensual — and the latter particularly by the Dravidians and Malays.

13. According to a too common opinion the norm is identical with the average, which amounts to saying that principle is reduced to fact or quality to quantity; mediocrity and ugliness become "reality." Now in ugliness the genius of the race is imprecise, for beauty alone is typical, it alone represents what is essential and intelligible.

The subtle and frenetic art of drumming, the passion of dance and its more or less sacred character and then the innocent pride, or proud innocence, of the naked body in both sexes — all these are features relating Africans to Dravidians and Balinese, except that among the Balinese the gamelan — an instrument of Mongolian type — replaces the Afro-Indian drum. As with the black people of Africa so also in the soul of the tropical Asiatics in question we find — though in lesser proportion and on a sacerdotal basis — something of the element "earth," something of its fertility, of its sensuality, its joy and its heavy indifference.

*
* *

According to a common error there exists an Italian, a German and a Russian "type" and so forth; in reality there is within each people a series of types, very divergent and of unequal importance, but all characteristic of that people; then there are types which can also be found among other peoples of the same race and, finally, one or more psychological types that are superimposed on these. For instance, in the series of types which are specifically Japanese one face may come much closer to a given Chinese type than to other Japanese faces; in the same way there are to be found among every people of the white race heads describable as "European" or "Arab" or "Hindu": the psychological significance of these conformations is generally quite secondary and is frequently neutralized by other factors, whereas a certain significance of "mental style" always remains valid. A similar error, much more widespread because bound up with political feelings and regional pride, is that which confuses a people with the political state in which the majority of them are living, and believes that groups accidentally found outside the frontiers of that state form other peoples. Thus only the inhabitants of France —

including groups foreign to the French people — are called "French" and only inhabitants of Germany are called "Germans," whereas in the past people rightly spoke of "the Germanys." The idea that the Walloons are different from the "French" is a case in point, as though Normans were not different from Gascons or as though some Germans (or rather "Germanics") in the South were not far more different from Prussians than from Alsatians or German Swiss, the Alemmanic tribe having been divided by several political frontiers as has also happened with the Bavaro-Austrian tribe. Regionalists also often cite mental differences due to secondary causes, exaggerating their importance; they forget, not merely that far greater differences occur within each country between different confessions, political parties, cultural levels and so forth, but also that political mentalities may be modified from one generation to another. In the same way, a pacific nature is often attributed to a particular people, or to an autonomous fraction of a people, just because they have no motive for making war, or are in no position to do so, or else because they only fight with "colored people" and so on; but there is no end to the confusions of this kind.

So far as real ethnic mentalities within Europe are concerned it is no exaggeration to say that Latins are rational and Germanics imaginative: generally speaking, an argument must be addressed either mainly to reason or to imagination according to whether it is intended for French or for German audiences. These traits may be good qualities — it would indeed be ungracious to reproach some Rhineland mystic for his spiritualized imagination — just as they can be defects, and in the latter case we say that a rationalism both "passional" and devoid of imagination, or in other words both arbitrary and sterile, has no greater worth than an intemperate imagination that is also passional; we are almost tempted to say that for the average Frenchman grandeur is folly, while for a

German folly is grandeur, rather as La Fontaine distinguished Frenchmen from Spaniards by saying of pride that "ours is much more stupid and theirs much more mad." And as for language, one knows that Latin words "define" whereas those of Germanic tongues "re-create" so that in the latter there is frequent onomatopoeia; Latin discerns, separates and isolates whereas Germanic languages are "existential" and symbolical, remaking things and suggesting qualities. A further example of these mental differences is furnished by German or Gothic script, which well expresses what the German genius has of imaginative, "vegetative," "warm" and "intimate" qualities (as shown in such words as *traut, heimatlich* and *geborgen*), whereas the Latin lettering by its mineral coldness and geometrical simplicity exteriorizes the clarity and somewhat unimaginative precision of the Romans. The importance of Gothic characters in the Middle Ages goes hand in hand with that of Germanic influence, against which the Renaissance battled and which the Reformation reaffirmed in its own fashion. The medieval cities of Northern Europe with their narrow houses, often outlandish in shape with the joinery showing, similarly express what is both of the intimate and of the whimsical in the Germanic soul.

*

* *

In art the white man, or at any rate the Occidental, tends to detach man from nature, even to oppose him to it; the yellow man remains in nature, which he spiritualizes and never destroys, so that the buildings of the yellow people always retain something of the spirit of the forest, and this is true even of Hinduized Indo-Chinese with whom a Hindu perspective has become integrated into a Mongolian way of seeing and feeling. In general it can be said that the material civilization of the yellow race remains close to the vegetable kingdom and to what is "natural," being associated with wood, bamboo and pottery rather than with stone, which the yellow man seems in general to distrust as being too "dead" and "ponderous" a material.[14] On the other hand, nothing is further from the genius of the yellow race than the muscular and dramatic nudes of the Westerners;[15] the yellow man sees primordial and celestial sublimity, not in the human body, but in virgin nature: the deities of the yellow race are like flowers, their faces like the full moon or the lotus; even the celestial nymphs of Buddhism combine their nudity — which still remains wholly Hindu in its marked sexuality and rhythm — with the flower-like grace lent them by the yellow genius. The serenity of Buddhas and the translucency of landscapes in the yellow man's art denote qualities of expression not to be found anywhere else in the same degree, qualities which are the very opposite of the tormented genius of the white peoples of Europe. Far Eastern painting has an aerial grace, the inimitable charm of a furtive and precious vision; by compensation, the terrifying presence of dragons, genii and demons adds to the art of the Far East a dynamic and flamboyant element.

14. The great stone temples of Angkor Wat and Borobudor are Indian monuments executed by yellow men Indianized.

15. There is a narrow-minded classicism which, because it has no objectively valid criterion and is as lacking in imagination as in intelligence and taste, sees in Chinese civilization only pettiness and routine: the Chinese are deemed inferior because they never produced a Michaelangelo or a Shakespeare, or because they did not create the Ninth Symphony and so on; now, if there is nothing Promethean in the greatness of the Chinese civilization, that is because it takes its stand on points where the classical prejudice cannot understand it; on the purely artistic level there are ancient bronzes which show more greatness and profundity than the whole of European nineteenth century painting. The first thing to be understood is that there is no true greatness apart from truth, and that truth certainly has no need of grandiloquent expressions. In these days we see a new reaction against classicism in the wider sense, but this reaction, far from being wholesome, on the contrary comes from below, according to the usual rhythm of a certain kind of "evolution."

Despite evident or possible analogies with the Western knight, the Japanese hero[16] keeps the laconic quality of the Mongol soul, while compensating this by a lyrical quality that is certainly moving but of a visual rather than auditive character and always inspired by nature. The Samurai is terse and subtle and does not forget, even in his sublimest moments, either practical sense or courtesy; he has impetuosity, a cold discipline and the delicacy both of an artist and of a Zen contemplative; the classical theater represents him as a sort of celestial insect whose astonishing capers and hieratic inflexibilities are far indeed from the hero of Greek or Shakespearean drama. In the yellow man's soul, which is little given to declamation, the smallest things unveil their secret greatness: a flower, a cup of tea, a precise and transparent brush-stroke; the greatness pre-exists in things, in their primary truth. This is also expressed in the music of the Far East: shrill sounds which form beads like the spume of a solitary cascade in a kind of morning melancholy; gong-strokes like the throbbing of a mountain of brass; chants surging from the intimacies of nature, but also from the sacred, from the solemn and golden dance of the Gods.

*

*   *

Despite the reservations which have to be made a priori, we should perhaps return at this point to the analogy established above between the three fundamental or "absolute" races on the one hand and the three visible elements on the

16. It is sometimes said that the Japanese have "European souls" which is just as false as asserting that the Russians have "Asiatic souls"; had the spirit of Japan been like that of the West, Mahayana Buddhism could never have been planted there, still less could it have been preserved intact; the same is true of Buddhist art, which found in Japan one of its most highly spiritual expressions.

other[17] by relating this to the Hindu theory of the three cosmic tendencies, the *gunas*. The Hindus attribute fire, which rises and gives light, to the ascending tendency, *sattva*; water, which is transparent and spreads horizontally, to the expansive tendency, *rajas;* and earth, which is heavy and opaque, to the descending or solidifying tendency, *tamas*. The precarious nature of the ascending tendency explains both the Greco-Roman and the modern deviations: that which is intellectual penetration and contemplativity among Hindus has become mental hypertrophy and inventiveness among Westerners; in both cases the accent is on "thought" in the widest sense, but the results are diametrically opposed. The white race is "speculative" both in the true and in the improper sense: it has strongly influenced the spirit of other races, not only through Brahminism, Buddhism, Islam and Christianity, but also through the modern deviation, without having been reciprocally influenced, except perhaps slightly. The yellow race is contemplative without laying stress on the dialectical element, that is, without feeling any need to clothe its wisdom in complex and highly mobile "mentalizations"; this race gave birth to Taoism, Confucianism and Shintoism; it created a writing unique in kind and an art that is original, profound and powerful, but it has not determined any foreign civilization; it has received a profound impression from Buddhism, a wisdom of white origin — it is not, of course, the wisdom that is racial but the human vehicle of the Revelation — while imprinting on

---

17. The two invisible elements, air and ether, are comprised in the visible elements, the former in a "horizontal" and "secondary" sense, the latter in a "vertical" or "primordial" sense; fire and water are absorbed into air which is as it were the basis on which they live, whereas ether penetrates all the other elements, being their *materia prima* or quintessence (*quinta essentia*). It must be clearly understood that in speaking of "elements" we are not thinking of chemical analysis but of the natural and immediate symbolism of appearances, which is perfectly valid and even "exact" from the point of view here adopted.

that tradition the mark of its own powerful and subtle genius.[18] The conquests of the yellow peoples swept along like a tidal wave throwing down everything in their path but not transforming their victims as did the white man's conquests;[19] the yellow races, whatever their impetuosity, "conserve" like water and do not "transmute" like fire; as conquerors they allow themselves to be absorbed by the vanquished of foreign civilizations. As for the black race, they are, as we have said, "existential" and this explains their passivity and inaptitude for radiating outwards, even within the fold of Islam; but this characteristic becomes qualitative and spiritual through the intervention of the contemplative element deep-rooted in every man and which gives its value to every natural determination.

It could also be said that the white and yellow races, insofar as they respectively correspond to the elements "fire" and "water," meet in the element "air." Air has the two qualities of lightness *(sattva)* and mobility *(rajas)*, whereas fire is characterized by luminosity *(sattva)* and heat

---

18. Here the pre-Columbian civilizations of America should also be mentioned, though in this case there was, alongside the Mongol element, an Atlantean element perhaps anterior to the great differentiation of races, or connected to the white people by an affinity with the ancient Egyptians and the primitive Berbers. America shows, both racially and culturally, a sort of mixture of Mongolian Siberia and ancient Egypt; hence the Shamanism, the conical tents, the leather robes adorned with fringes, the magical drums, the long hair, the feathers and, in the South, the pyramids, the colossal temples with their static form, the hieroglyphs and the mummies. Between the three great races of humanity there are doubtless not only types due to admixtures but also, it would seem, types which remained more or less undifferentiated; it can also be supposed that, while primordial humanity did not as yet know different races, it sporadically included highly differentiated types which as it were prefigured the races of today.

19. Caesar Romanized Gaul, the Moslems Islamized parts of Africa, Europe and Asia and the Europeans have Europeanized America, but the Mongols never "Mongolized" any country. Their spiritual genius is too implicit to be able to so deeply affect other races.

(rajas) and water by fluidity *(rajas)* and weight or passivity *(tamas)*; but there is also destructiveness *(tamas)* in fire and transparency *(sattva)* in water, so that inasmuch as "transparency" predominates in the yellow race, in its contemplativity and in the art in which this quality is materialized, it comes "nearer to Heaven" than the white race inasmuch as the latter takes on the aspect of destructiveness *(tamas)*. The element "earth" has the two aspects of heaviness or immobility *(tamas)* and fertility *(rajas)* but also adds to these, through minerals, a luminous possibility which might be termed "crystallinity" *(sattva)*; the spirituality of black men often has a static purity and turns to account all that the black mentality contains of the stable, the simple and the concrete. That which is "inertia" (earth) in the black man becomes "equilibrium" (water) in the yellow man, and one of the most striking traits of that race is indeed its faculty of holding the balance between extremes. As for the instability (fire) of the white man, it is significant that the Hindus have neutralized this by the caste system in order to obviate from the outset the danger of deviation inherent in the fiery cosmic quality *(sattva)*;[20] among the Semites, and among Europeans influenced by the Semitic spirit, this instability is compensated by religious dogmatism.[21] Ether has the intrinsic quality of principial immuta-

---

20. We refer here to a theory according to which fire, inasmuch as it tends to rise and to illuminate, corresponds to *sattva*, whereas water, inasmuch as it spreads horizontally and fertilizes can be assimilated to *rajas*, earth then corresponding to *tamas* owing to its inertia and compressive power; but it goes without saying that in another respect fire is *rajas* through its consuming and passionate heat, in which case light alone corresponds to *sattva*; this is the trend not of the visible elements — fire, earth — but of the sensory functions of the sun-fire; luminosity, heat and negatively, darkness. Pure luminosity is cold through its transcendence; darkness is cold only through privation.

21. As for those groups of yellow and black people who are adherents of Semitic religions, dogma appears in their case, not in its stabilizing function, but in its simplifying function, the danger for them being, not one of ideological divagation, but of ignorance and materialism.

bility or ipseity *(sattva)* and the extrinsic aspects of differentiation *(rajas)* and solidification *(tamas)*; in this play of correspondencies it would then represent primordial man or — by derivation — man as such. This "alchemy" will not seem strange to our regular readers and will above all show them — if there is need for such demonstration — that in each racial determination there is a positive aspect which, in case of need, is able to neutralize a baneful aspect.

In any case, if the white race can claim a relative preeminence, it can do so only through the Hindu group which in a way perpetuates the primordial state of the Indo-Europeans and, in a wider sense, that of white men as a whole. The Hindus surpass every other human group by their extraordinary contemplativity and the metaphysical genius resulting from this; but the yellow race is in its turn far more contemplative than the Western branch of the white race, and this makes it possible, looking at things as a whole, to speak of spiritual superiority in the traditional East, whether white or yellow, also including in this superiority the Messianic and Prophetic outlook of the Semites, which runs parallel with the Aryan *avatāric* outlook. All these facts are now called into question because of the modern spirit, which has the power so to shake or upset all values that a natural propensity to spirituality may lose all its efficacy, and such that spirituality may in the end come to be actualized in a quarter where it could least have been expected. This leads us once again to underline the conditional nature of all hereditary superiority: if one takes account of the part played by religions and ideological influences as well as of the interplay of compensations in both space and time, if one observes, for instance, that some group held to be barbarian may be incontestably superior to some other group held to be civilized (not to mention the possibility of a personal superiority of individuals of any group whatsoever) then one must recognize that the question of racial superiority is in practice pointless.

*

*   *

It will have been gathered from what has been said above that for us the question is not: "What is our racial heritage?" but rather: "What are we making of that heritage?" To talk about a racial value is, for the individual, quite meaningless, for the existence of Christ or of the Vedantic doctrine adds nothing to the value of a white man with a base nature any more than the barbarism of certain African tribes takes anything away from a black man of saintly soul; and as for the effective value, not of a race, but of an ethnic atavism, this is a question of "spiritual alchemy," not of scientific or racist dogmatism.

In one respect the metaphysical reason for races is that differences cannot be merely qualitative as in the case of castes; differences can and must also arise "horizontally," from the point of view simply of modes and not of essences. There cannot be only differences between light and darkness, there must also be differences of color.

If each caste is in some way to be found in the other castes, the same thing can be said of races, for the same reasons and apart from any question of racial admixtures. But besides castes and races there are also four temperaments, which Galen relates to the four sensible elements, and the astrological types, which are related to the planets of our system. All these types or possibilities are present in the human substance and form the individual by determining him in many different ways: to know the aspects of man is one way of better knowing oneself.

Races exist and we cannot ignore them, less than ever now that the time of closed universes has come to an end and with it the right to purely conventional simplifications; in any case what it is above all important to understand is that racial determination can only be relative, man thus determined never ceasing to be man as such.

The modern movement towards uniformity, which causes the world to become smaller and smaller, seems able to attenuate racial differences, at any rate at the mental level and without speaking of ethnic mixtures. In this there is nothing surprising if one reflects that this standardizing civilization is at the opposite pole from any higher synthesis, based as it is solely on man's earthly needs; human animality provides in principle a rather facile ground for mutual understanding and favors the breaking down of traditional civilizations under auspices of a quantitative and spiritually inoperative "culture." But the fact of thus depending on what gives mankind a "low level solidarity" presupposes the detaching of the masses, who are intellectually passive and unconscious, from the elites who legitimately represent them and in consequence also incarnate both the tradition, insofar as it is adapted to a given race, and the genius of that race in the most lofty sense.[22]

*

* *

Let us take the opportunity to insert here, alongside these considerations about races and not unconnected with them, some remarks on the opposition — true or false — between West and East. First of all, there is in both cases an inner opposition between the sacred patrimony and whatever actively or passively moves away from that patrimony; this shows that the distinction between East and West is not absolute, that there is a "Western East" as there was — and

22. If we write "elites" in the plural it is not because we believe in the existence of some other elite besides that which is intellectual or spiritual — without a foundation of truth and thus intellectuality no spirituality can exist — but solely in order to show that the elite includes modes and levels which run through a people as arteries run through a body; if the elite is first of all sacerdotal in substance, it is nonetheless true that sections of the elite are to be found at all levels of society, just as inversely, there is no sacerdotal body without its Pharisees, but this fact in no way abolishes the normal hierarchy.

169

perhaps still is within certain frameworks — an "Eastern West," as at Mount Athos or in some other relatively isolated phenomenon. In considering the East we must thus start by differentiating — if we are to avoid inextricable contradictions — between Orientals who owe nothing, or almost nothing, to the West and have every right and reason to resist it, and those who on the contrary owe, or imagine they owe, everything to it, but who also too readily spend their time in enumerating the colonialist crimes of Europe, as though Europeans were the only men to have conquered countries and exploited peoples. The blind haste with which westernized Orientals of every political color press on with the westernizing of the East proves beyond all question how thoroughly they themselves are convinced of the superiority of modern Western civilization, that very civilization which engendered colonialism as also the cult of machines and Marxism. Now there are few things so absurd as the anti-Westernism of those who are themselves westernized. A choice must be made: either that civilization is worthy of adoption, in which case Europeans are supermen to whom unbounded gratitude is owed, or else Europeans are malefactors deserving contempt and then they and their civilization fall together and there is no reason for imitating them. But in practice the West is being completely and whole-heartedly imitated even in the most pointless of its caprices; far from limiting themselves to modern armaments for purposes of legitimate defense or to an equipment of economic tools capable of meeting the situations created by an overpopulation that is itself partly due to the biological crimes of modern science, Eastern nations adopt the very soul of the antitraditional West to the point of seeking in the "science of religions," in psychoanalysis and even in surrealism the keys to the age-old wisdom of the East. In a word, they believe in the superiority of the West but reproach Westerners for having believed in it.

Let us leave this paradoxical aspect of modernism and inquire of the timeless soul of Asia and Africa. In the eyes of non-Western men who remain faithful to their traditions, what makes Western colonialism more odious than other yokes physically more cruel, is precisely those characteristics which are found only in modern civilization: firstly a materialism that is not merely confined to the physical realm but also claims the realm of the spirit — materialism, *de jure* and not only *de facto* — secondly the mixture of hypocrisy[23] and perfidy which stems from this materialism and thirdly the fact that everything is made trivial and ugly; but above all it is their political invincibility and cultural inassimilability which confer on the "whites" — in the conventional sense of the term — a character never before seen, something as it were extra-human or almost "Martian."[24] Neither Mongols nor Moslems showed this strange

23. It is, for instance, a biased hypocrisy to call a people "barbarous" because they "did such and such things" and to deny them on that account rights considered to be elementary, while attributing the same kind of actions in other favored cases to the "period" or to "circumstances," according to whether they be past or present. Again, when people cannot avoid applying the term "barbarism" to European adversaries, the same hypocrisy often makes them add the epithet "Asiatic" as though the Europeans as such — considered, that is, apart from any affinity with the rest of humanity — were incapable of evil-doing.

24. The metropolitans take a far too summary view of their colonies in the sense that they think only of "benefits conferred" — or what seem so in their eyes — and forget, not only the scale of values of the foreign civilization, but also the special mentality of the colonial settlers, which is necessarily deformed by their own abnormal and psychologically "unhealthy" situation. The question is endlessly discussed whether the colonial peoples are "good" or "bad," "grateful" or "ungrateful," and it is forgotten that, being men, they cannot fail to have certain reactions in certain circumstances. Colonial settlers inevitably have an absurd superiority complex, as Lyautey noted with regret, and the "natives" cannot fail to suffer because of it; there are some things in the human soul which cannot be replaced by means of roads and hospitals and it is astonishing that Europeans, who are such "idealists," should be so slow to perceive this. If Europeans believe that they offer to those they "protect" liberties they never knew, they do not take into account that these liberties exclude other modes of liberty of which they themselves

171

antitraditional spirit; their military power was not absolute; Mongols and Manchus were turned into Chinese, other Mongols were absorbed by Islam or, in the West, by Christianity. The conquering thrust of the Moslems finally came up against its natural limits, but what is far more important is that the Islamic mentality was traditional and in its deepest tendencies reconcilable with Hinduism: Moslem spirituality could even give a fresh impetus to Vaishnavite mysticism, just as Buddhism had been able, a few centuries earlier, to revivify certain aspects of Hindu spirituality. The very least one can say is that the modern spirit includes nothing of the kind — given its professed principles and its tendencies and in spite of current illusions — and that the Western threat to the most sacred things of the East on the contrary knows no limits, as is proven precisely by the antitraditional spirit of "young Orientals" or by what comes to the same thing, the present suicide of the East.

For "youth" the final humiliation is to be weak and thus open to "colonization"; weakness is then often seen as synonymous with tradition, as if no question of truth need arise either in the evaluation of Western strength or in the interpretation of traditional values. What is "true" is strength, even if it leads to hell; ancient corruption is succeeded by an angry and even diabolical virtue; they would "liberate" a people even at the price of what gives meaning to its existence and readily accept the idea that "we must move with the times," as if there could be an imperative requiring man to abdicate his intelligence, or indeed permitting him to do so. If error is inevitable, so, just as much, is intellectual opposition to error, and this,

hardly conceive any longer; they give good things, but at the same time impose their own conceptions of what is good, and this comes back to the ancient saying that might is always right. This mentality first dams up and then releases in the colonial people all that is basest in collective man; everything possible has been done to compromise the tradition, whose ruin was always wished for, and then people are astonished at the evil springing from its disintegration.

quite apart from any question of what may be opportune or presently effective; truth is good, not because it is opportune or efficacious, but because it is true, not forgetting that truth coincides with reality and that, therefore, *vincit omnia Veritas.*

All these considerations call to mind the disappointment felt by some when they see how easily age-old traditions crumble despite the contemplative mentality of the peoples concerned, a mentality which they had believed would offer sure guarantees. But two things are forgotten: in the first place, there are not only contemplative Orientals and "activist" Westerners, there are also, whatever the traditional setting, men who are spiritual and men who are worldly; in the second place, only a minority in any civilization consciously and actively participates in the spirit of the tradition, the majority remaining more or less "fallow," open, that is, to receive influences of no matter what kind. It is well known how easily many Hindus, Malays and Chinese accepted a spiritual form so foreign to them as Islam, and this is proof of a certain detachment from their native traditions; when there is joined to this detachment — or this passivity, as the case may be — a materialistic and worldly spirit (and God knows how many Orientals can be "in fact" materialists) there is no reason to be astonished when traditions are abandoned and materialistic ideologies adopted. Worldliness in the widest sense, love of pleasures or greed of gain, or in short the overestimation of the things of this world, has always been a door open to error; an intellectual capacity is far from being absolute as a criterion and absolute guarantee. Here it should be added that the spiritual minority which consciously and "actively" participates in the tradition is to be found in every layer of society, and this amounts to saying conversely that "passive," "unconscious" and "worldly" people are also to be found everywhere.

In an analogous order of ideas we should wish to say this: whatever may be the defects of modern man it cannot be said that he enjoys no kind of at least virtual or conditional superiority over "ancient" man, even if it be relative, which we could specify in the following way: suppose a Western man of today came to recognize all the errors that surround him and suppose he could return to the Middle Ages or live in no matter what wholly traditional world and adopt its ways of thinking and acting, even then, despite everything, he would never become quite a medieval man; his spirit would retain the imprint of experiences unknown to the generality of non-modern men. Here we have in mind especially a critical sense which is developed only thanks to obstacles and of which a traditional world is ignorant because certain obstacles never appear there; certain functions of intelligence are hardly ever deployed except in struggle and disappointment. In traditional worlds a certain tendency to exaggeration and to its accompanying illogicalities, as well as to facile prejudices, is inevitable and is explained precisely by the too "compact" character of ideas and tastes; in other words, there are realms of his being in which ancient man never suffered just as there are things he never saw called into question. Man is made in such a way that he is never fully actualized within the limits of his possibilities except with the help of constraints, otherwise he would be perfect; where there is no brake there is exaggeration and unconsciousness. If what has just been said cannot be applied to the chosen vessels of the ancient wisdoms, it does apply to the common run of men and it is they who necessarily give their imprint to the whole civilization.

*
* *

In conclusion let us return to the question of race: if ethnic differences only too often provide illusory motives for hatred, more normally they include reasons for love: by this we mean that foreign races have something complementary in relation to ourselves without there being in principle any "lack" in us or in them either. Assuredly it would be senseless to love a whole race or to love some individual just because he belongs to a foreign race; but it is clear that one could not understand some particular racial beauty without understanding and consequently "loving" the race which is its substance — any more than one could love a woman without loving femininity — and this is all the more true on the level of the soul: the qualities which make a particular human being lovable at the same time make the genius of his race lovable. In the final analysis one can only love the Self, for there is nothing else in the Universe to love; now a man of another race, supposing he corresponds to us by analogy or by complementarism, is like a forgotten aspect of ourselves and thus also like a rediscovered mirror of God.

The Sacred Pipe
of the Red Indians

It will doubtless come as something of a surprise to Indian readers* to find here a chapter on the tradition of the North American Indians figuring side by side with more familiar subjects: this fact calls for a few words of explanation by way of showing that this unexpected reference to a rarely appreciated form of spirituality has been introduced advisedly and for reasons that are not foreign to the general purpose of this book.

There is always something to be gained from the consideration, across differences of form, race and historical background, of the same great metaphysical truths to which one's own tradition is one's most directly accessible witness: every concordant testimony will serve to reinforce one's own deepest convictions. Such a force of example will lose none of its efficacy when it is offered, as in the present case, by the survivors of a proud and heroic people who, with a tenacity almost unparalleled, have managed to preserve, if precariously, the essentials of a metaphysical doctrine of the most profound character, together with the sacred rites serving as its vehicle among men, in the face of adverse

* Translator's note: Readers are asked to keep in mind that this collection of essays was first published in India and that this revised translation is being republished there.

conditions such as, for any people less strong minded, would long since have made them give up in despair. The truth is that the Red Indians, even in defeat and despoilment, have never suffered from a sense of inferiority in regard to the white civilization that overwhelmed them; in this respect they differ from many who, seemingly, have been far more fortunately placed. Denied the things usually associated with the word *svarāj* the Red Indian has kept its deeper meaning alive in his own heart; and that is why he also has something to offer to all who still value that spiritual freedom without which all other so-called freedoms are but an empty shell.

However, there are also other and more particular reasons why the wisdom of the Red Indians should be of interest to Hindus and these rest upon the truly primordial character of the tradition in question, which in many of its expressions as also in its manner of reading deep truths through the signs of Nature is highly reminiscent of India in Vedic times. Similarly, the cosmological lore of the American Indians exhibits many striking analogies with the corresponding Hindu doctrine, a parallelism that is all the more suggestive inasmuch as there is no known connection between the two forms — unless perhaps one were to hark back to an original northern home of traditional wisdom, long prior to all recorded history. What is however certain is that the American Indians, though accidentally so named by the early European invaders who in sailing Westward had thought to open a new route to Asia and its wealth — cupidity was, with them, a dominant motive — well deserve the title in virtue of a spiritual kinship that makes all true traditions one and all noble peoples *Aryas*.**

*
* *

** These introductory remarks were added by the translators of the first edition of *Language of the Self* (Ganesh, 1959).

The Indians of North America[1] possess, in their tradition, a symbol and "means of grace" of the first importance: the Sacred Pipe, which represents not only a doctrinal synthesis, both concise and complex, but also a ritual instrument around which centers their whole spiritual and social life. To describe the symbolism of the Sacred Pipe and of its rite is thus, in a certain sense, to expound the sum of Indian wisdom. It will not be necessary to treat this subject here in all its fullness; to do so would be difficult inasmuch as the Red Indian tradition varies considerably in its forms of expression (as may be seen for example in the myth of the origin of the Calumet and in the symbolism of colors), such variations being due to the scattering of the tribes in the course of the centuries;[2] we will therefore dwell rather upon the fundamental aspects of this wisdom which, as such, remain always the same beneath the variety of the ways in which they are expressed. We will use, however, in preference to others, the doctrinal symbols found among the Sioux, the nation which can be considered, in certain respects, as "central" among Indian peoples, and to which belonged Hehaka Sapa — Black Elk — the venerable author of *The Sacred Pipe*.[3] The teachings of this sage have been particularly precious to us, as much from the point of view of doctrine as from that of living spirituality in our times.

1. Or rather, to be more precise: the Indians of the plains and forests which stretch from the Rocky Mountains (and even from farther West) to the Atlantic Ocean.

2. The same thing is true of Hinduism and perhaps of every tradition which has a mythological form; in Hinduism the same symbols may vary considerably from region to region: the same term may signify a fundamental reality in one place and a secondary aspect of the same reality elsewhere.

3. *The Sacred Pipe: Black Elk's Account of the Seven Rites of the Oglala Sioux,* by Joseph Epes Brown. Norman, University of Oklahoma Press, 1975. Black Elk died in 1950 on Pine Ridge Reservation (South Dakota).

While the Indians of North America are one of the races which have been most studied by ethnographers; it cannot be said that everything about them is fully known, for the simple reason that ethnography does not embrace all possible forms of knowledge — any more than do other ordinary sciences — and therefore cannot possibly be regarded as a general key. There is in fact a sphere which by definition is beyond the reach of ordinary science ("outward" or "profane" science, that is to say), but which is the very basis of every civilization: this is spirituality — the knowledge of Divine Reality and of the means of realizing It, in some degree or other, in oneself. Clearly no one can understand any one form of spirituality without knowing spirituality in itself;[4] to be able to know the wisdom of a people we must first of all possess the keys to such wisdom, and these indispensable keys are to be found, not in any subsidiary branch of learning, but in intellectuality at its purest and most universal level. To disallow that which is the very essence of all true wisdom is to bar ourselves in advance from understanding any wisdom at all; in other words, the forms of a known wisdom are the necessary keys to the understanding of any other wisdom as yet unknown.

Some writers feel the need to question whether the idea of God is really present in the Red Indian religion, because they think they see in it a sort of "pantheism" or "immanentism"; but this misunderstanding is simply due to the fact that most of the Indian terms for the Divinity refer to all Its possible aspects, and not merely, as is the case with the word "God," (at least in practice) to Its personal aspect alone; *Wakan-Tanka* (the "Great Spirit") is God not only as Creator and Lord but also as Impersonal Essence.

---

4. It is quite evident that a knowledge of skull shapes, idioms and folklore customs in no wise qualifies a person for an intellectual penetration of ideas and symbols. Certain ethnologists believe themselves justified in calling "vague" every conception they themselves fail to understand.

Objections are sometimes raised to the name "Great Spirit" as a translation of the Sioux word *Wakan-Tanka,* and of similar terms in other Indian languages; but although *Wakan-Tanka* (and the terms which correspond to it) can also be translated by "Great Mystery" or "Great Mysterious Power" (or even "Great Medicine"), and although "Great Spirit" is no doubt not absolutely adequate, it nonetheless serves quite well enough and in any case conveys the meaning in question better than any other term; it is true that the word "spirit" is rather indefinite, but it has for that very reason the advantage of implying no restriction, and this is exactly what the "polysynthetic" term *Wakan* requires. The expression "Great Mystery" which has been suggested by some as a translation of *Wakan-Tanka* (or of the analogous terms, such as *Wakonda* or *Manitu,* in other Indian languages) is no better than "Great Spirit" at expressing the idea in question: besides, what matters is not whether the term corresponds exactly to what we mean by "Spirit," but whether the ideas expressed by the Red Indian term may be translated by "Spirit" or not.

The Sioux make a clear distinction between the essential aspects of *Wakan-Tanka*: *Tunkashila* (Grandfather) is *Wakan-Tanka* insofar as He is beyond all manifestation, and even beyond all quality or determination whatsoever; *Ate* (Father) on the other hand is God in Act: the Creator, the Nourisher, the Destroyer. Analogously they make a distinction, as regards the Earth, between *Unchi* (Grandmother) and *Ina* (Mother): *Unchi* is the Substance of all things (*Mula-Prakriti*), whereas *Ina* is her creative act (considered here as "childbearing"), which conjointly with "inspiration" by *Ate,* produces all beings — *Prakriti* viewed in her relation to *Purusha.*

It is through the animal species and the phenomena of Nature that the Indian contemplates the angelic Essences and the Divine Qualities; in this connection we will quote from one of Joseph Epes Brown's letters: "It is often difficult for those who look on the tradition of the red man from the outside or through the 'educated' mind, to understand their preoccupation with the animals, and with all things in the Universe. But for these people, as of course for all traditional peoples, every created object is important simply because they know the metaphysical correspondence between this world and the 'Real World.' No object is for them what it appears to be, but it is simply the pale shadow of a Reality. It is for this reason that every created object is *wakan*, holy, and has a power according to the loftiness of the spiritual reality that it reflects; thus many objects possess negative powers as well as those which are positive and good, and every object is treated with respect, for the particular 'power' that it possesses can be transferred into man — of course they know that everything in the Universe has its counterpart in the soul of man. The Indian humbles himself before the whole of creation, especially when 'lamenting' (that is, when he ritually invokes the 'Great Spirit' in solitude), because all visible things were created before him and, being older than he, deserve respect (this priority of created things may also be taken as a symbol of the Priority of the Principle); but although the last of created things, man is also the first, since he alone may know the Great Spirit *(Wakan-Tanka)*."[5]

5. "The Indian's religion is generally spoken of as Nature and Animal worship. The term seems too broadcast and indiscriminate. Careful inquiry and observation fail to show that the Indian actually worships the objects which are set up or mentioned by him in his ceremonies. The earth, the four winds, the sun, moon and stars, the stones, the water, the various animals, are all exponents of a mysterious life and power. . . ." (Alice C. Fletcher, *The Elk Mystery or Festival.*) — "A thing is not only what it is visibly, but also what it represents. Natural or artificial objects are not for the primitive, as they can be for us, arbitrary 'symbols' of some other and higher reality, but actual manifestations of this reality: the eagle or the lion, for example, is not so much a symbol or image of the Sun as it is the Sun in a likeness (the form being more important than the nature in which it may be manifested); and in the same way every house is the world in a likeness, and every altar is situated at the center of the earth; it is only

This will help to explain in what way every "typical" thing, that is, everything that manifests an "essence," is *wakan*, sacred. To believe that God is the sun is certainly an altogether "pagan" error (and one that is quite foreign to Red Indian thought), but it is just as absurd (at least, metaphysically) to believe that the sun is simply and solely an incandescent mass or, in other words, that in no way whatsoever is it God. We might express the idea like this: *wakan* is whatever conforms integrally to its proper "genius," its *svadharma*; the Principle is *Wakan-Tanka*, namely: what is absolutely "Self"; on the other hand a sage is he who is wholly in conformity with his "genius" or with his "essence," with that which is none other than the "Great Spirit" or the "Great Mystery." *Wakan* is what enables us to apprehend directly the Divine Reality; a man is *wakan* when his soul manifests the Divine with the spontaneous and flashing evidence of the wonders of Nature: the elements, the sun, lightning, the eagle. . . . That is why cowardice (a kind of forsaking one's "personality") is the foremost sin; and that also explains the Indian "individualism," either seeming or real.

As to the knowledge of the "Great Spirit" which man alone of all earthly creation may attain to, Black Elk once defined it as follows: "I am blind and do not see the things

because 'we' are more interested in what things are than in what they mean, more interested in particular facts than in universal ideas, that this is 'inconceivable' to us. Descent from a totem animal is not, then, what it appears to the anthropologist, a literal absurdity, but a descent from the Sun, the Progenitor and *Prajapati* of all, in that form in which he revealed himself whether in vision or in dream, to the founder of the clan . . . So that, as Lévy-Bruhl says of such symbols, 'very often it is not their purpose to "represent" their prototype to the eye, but to facilitate a participation,' and that 'if it is their essential function to "represent," in the full sense of the word, invisible beings or objects, and to make their presence effective, it follows that they are not necessarily reproductions or likenesses of these beings or objects.' " (Ananda K. Coomaraswamy, *Figures of Speech or Figures of Thought,* London, Luzac & Co., 1946.)

of this world; but when the Light comes from Above, it enlightens my heart and I can see, for the Eye of my heart *(Chante Ista)* sees everything. The heart is a sanctuary at the center of which there is a little space, wherein the Great Spirit dwells, and this is the Eye *(Ista)*. This is the Eye of the Great Spirit by which He sees all things and through which we see Him. If the heart is not pure, the Great Spirit cannot be seen, and if you should die in this ignorance, your soul cannot return immediately to the Great Spirit, but it must be purified by wandering about in the world *(samsāra)*. In order to know the center of the heart where the Great Spirit dwells you must be pure and good, and live in the manner that the Great Spirit has taught us. The man who is thus pure contains the Universe in the pocket of his heart *(Chante Ognaka)*."[6]

All we have said so far may be taken as an illustration of the red race's polysynthetic genius, which makes itself evident most directly in these people's languages: just as the verb embraces in itself all the different elements that go to make up the sentence, so the fundamental conception of the "Great Spirit" embraces all the different elements that go to make up the thought, which means that the Universe is considered only as it relates to God, and this easily explains why the Indians are suspected of pantheism — always most undiscerningly — by people who have received a philosophical, rationalistic and conceptualistic education. Nothing illustrates better the polysynthetic perspective than the verses of the *Rigveda* (X.90) in which the world is likened to a part of Universal Man, *Purusha*, the victim of the Primordial Sacrifice whence all beings originate: "This world is nought but *Purusha*. . . . Three quarters of him rose

---

6. As is often the case, the deep-rooted agreement of the traditional doctrines shows itself here even in forms and details. We might recall also the "Eye of the Heart" in the Plotinian doctrine as also in the Augustinian doctrine; no less remarkable is the close parallelism with the description of *Brahma-pura* as given in the *Chhandogya Upanishad*, for instance.

aloft, one quarter of him spread in this world so as to pervade all beings, the animate and the inanimate."

The Sacred Pipe is as it were the central expression of this polysynthesis: it is the synthesis of all knowledge — the content of all knowledge being *Wakan-Tanka,* Who alone "is."

*

* *

The Calumet was revealed, or "sent down from Heaven"; its coming into this world is supernatural, as the sacred narratives bear witness.

Before giving a summary account of the symbolism of the Calumet, we cannot do better than quote the explanation which was given of it by Black Elk in the first book whereby he became known to the outside world:[7] "I fill this sacred Pipe with the bark of the red willow; but before we smoke it, you must see how it is made and what it means. These four ribbons hanging here on the stem are the four quarters of the universe. The black one is for the west where the thunder beings live to send us rain; the white one for the north, whence comes the great white cleansing wind; the red one for the east, whence springs the light and where the morning star lives to give men wisdom; the yellow for the south, whence come the summer and the power to grow. But these four spirits are only one Spirit after all, and this eagle feather here is for that One, which is like a father, and also it is for the thoughts of men that should rise high as eagles do. Is not the sky a father and the earth a mother, and are not all living things with feet or wings or roots their children? And this hide upon the mouthpiece here, which should be bison hide, is for the earth, from whence we came and at whose breast we suck as babies all our lives, along with all the animals and birds and trees and grasses. And

7. *Black Elk Speaks,* New York, Washington Square Press, 1972.

because it means all this, and more than any man can understand, the Pipe is holy."

When the Indian performs the rite of the Calumet, he greets the sky, the earth and the four cardinal points, either by offering them the Pipe, stem forward (in accordance with the ritual of the Sioux, for example), or by blowing the smoke towards the different directions, and sometimes also towards the "central fire"[8] burning in front of him; the order of these gestures may vary, but their static plan remains always the same, since it is the doctrinal figure of which the rite is to be the enactment.

In keeping with certain ritual practices, we will begin our enumeration with the West: the West Wind brings with it, as we have already seen, thunder and rain, that is, Revelation and also Grace; the North Wind purifies and gives strength; from the East comes Light, that is, Knowledge, and these, according to the Indian perspective, go together with Peace; the South is the source of Life and Growth; it is there that the "Good Red Road" begins, the way of welfare and felicity. The Universe thus depends on four primordial determinations — Water, Cold, Light, Warmth; the first of these, Water, is none other than the positive aspect of darkness which should normally stand in opposition to light, just as cold is the opposite of warmth; the positive aspect of darkness is in fact its quality of shade which gives protection against the parching strength of the sun and which produces or favors moisture; the sky must grow dark

8. "The fire of his council or of his great medicine lodge, as some of his songs bear witness, is the oldest of all: it is practically the same as what the Greek philosophers of the school of Pythagoras named Hestia, which burns at the center of the earth. It is in this central fire that he takes part by mingling his breath with the fire of the sacred tobacco, and it is the same fire which rises with its smoke towards the zenith of the universe or sinks to the nadir, touching the earth, or joins the four winds which, filled with the beautiful life of the high heavens, blow round about our human habitation." (Hartly Burr Alexander, *The Art and Philosophy of the North American Indians*, Paris, E. Leroux, 1926.)

before it can give rain, and God manifests Anger (thunder) before granting Grace, of which rain is the natural symbol. As to Cold ("the sanctifying and purifying wind which gives strength"), its positive aspect is purity so that the Purity of the North may be placed in opposition to the Warmth of the South, just as the Rain of the West is opposable to the Light from the East; the connection between Cold and Purity is evident: inanimate, cold things, that is, minerals — unlike animate, warm beings — are not subject to corruption. The Light of the East is, as we have already said, Knowledge; and Warmth is Life and therefore Love, and also Goodness, Beauty, Happiness.

Before going further, we may reply to an objection which might arise from the fact that in the Sioux mythology, the Four Winds seem to correspond to a rather secondary function of the Divinity, which is here divided into four Aspects, each of which contains four subdivisions. The Sioux doctrine, by a remarkable derogation of the ordinary mythological hierarchy, gives a preeminence to these four Principles over the other Divinities, showing thereby very clearly that, in the rite of the Calumet or rather in the perspective that goes with it, the cardinal points represent the four essential Divine Manifestations.

It should moreover never be forgotten that among other Indians this symbolism takes on forms very different from those to be found among the Sioux: thus (to cite a single example) the four Principles are symbolized among the Arapaho by four Old Men sprung from the Sun who watch over the inhabitants of the terrestrial world and to whom are attributed symbolically the day (South-East), summer (South-West), night (North-West) and winter (North-East). Finally, it is worth noting that the Quaternary is often considered in the last analysis as constituting a Duodecad, each element being considered under three aspects, quite apart from the vertical axis of Heaven and Earth which adds two new elements to the Quaternary, though these are not of the same order. We cannot dwell on all of these variations, and we need only stress the fact that they are independent of the Quaternary Principle which alone concerns us here.

Coming back now to the consideration of the four Principles: it would also be possible to speak of the four "cosmic Places" in the following terms, here again, as always, starting from the West and moving towards the North: Moisture, Cold, Drought, Warmth; the West's negative aspect, the correlative of moisture, is darkness, and the East's positive aspect, the correlative of drought, is light. The Thunderbird (*Wakinyan-Tanka*) whose abode is in the West, and who protects the earth and its vegetation against drought and death, is said to flash lightning from its eyes and to thunder with its wings;[9] the analogy with the Revelation on Mount Sinai, which was accompanied by "thunders and lightnings, and a thick cloud" (Exodus 19:16) is all the more striking in that this Revelation took place on a rock, while in the Indian mythology it is precisely the Rock which is connected with the Thunderbird, as we shall see from what follows. As to the symbolic connection between Revelation and the West, it may seem unusual and even paradoxical, but it should always be remembered that in Indian symbolism the cardinal points are necessarily positive in their

9. According to Iroquois mythology, "Hino, the Spirit of Thunder . . . is the guardian of Heaven. Armed with a powerful bow and arrows of fire (flashes of lightning), he destroys all harmful things. His consort 'The Rainbow'. . . Oshadagea, 'The Great Eagle of the Dew,' is also at the service of Hino. He lives in the Heaven of the West and carries in the hollow of his back a lake of dew. When the maleficent fire sprites destroy all the earth's greenery, Oshadagea takes flight and from his outspread wings the beneficent moisture flows drop by drop." (Max Fauconnet: *Mythologies des deux Ameriques,* in *Mythologie Generale* of the Librairie Larousse.) — This association of the lightning with the Thunderbird is all the more remarkable in that the most diverse traditions connect lightning with Revelation, just as they connect rain with Grace. The eagle and the lightning belong to the same universal symbolism; hence in the Christian tradition the association of the eagle with Saint John, Revealer of the Apocalypse and "Son of Thunder."

meaning: thus, as we have already said, the West is not the opposite of the East, not Darkness and ignorance, but the positive complement of the East, that is rain and Grace. It might also seem surprising that the Indian tradition should establish a symbolical link between the West Wind, bearer of thunder and rain, and the Rock which is an angelic or semi-divine personification of a cosmic Aspect of *Wakan-Tanka*; but this connection is admissible, for in the rock are united the same complementary aspects as in the thunderstorm: the terrible aspect by reason of its destructive hardness (the rock is, for the Indians, a symbol of destruction — hence his stone weapons of which the connection with thunderbolts is obvious), and the aspect of Grace through its giving birth to springs which, like the rain, quench the thirst of the land.[10]

There still remains something to be said about the association of the Winds with the cardinal points: these four Winds are the Productive Forces (in the sense of the Sanskrit word *Shakti*) of the Quarters of the World, and they are

---

10. It should be mentioned here that in the world of the Red Indian the "rocks," namely the Rocky Mountains, lie to the West and give birth to a number of rivers by which the plains are fertilized; this is an example, among many others, of sacred geography. — "When a vision comes from the thunder beings of the West, it comes with terror like a thunderstorm; but when the storm of vision has passed, the world is greener and happier; for whenever the truth of vision comes upon the world, it is like a rain. The world, you see, is happier after the terror of the storm" (*Black Elk Speaks*, op. cit.). — Asceticism springs from the same cosmic connection between terror and Grace, and here again the Indian tradition does not differ from other forms of spirituality: " 'To make medicine' is to engage upon a special period of fasting, thanksgiving, prayer and self-denial, even of self-torture. . . . The procedure is entirely a devotional exercise. The purpose is to subdue the passions of the flesh and to improve the spiritual self. The bodily abstinence and the mental concentration upon lofty thoughts cleanses both the body and the soul. . . . Then the individual mind gets closer towards conformity with the mind of the Great Medicine above us." (Wooden Leg — a Cheyenne Indian — in his book: *A Warrior who Fought Custer*, Lincoln, University of Nebraska Press, 1962.)

conceived of as encircling the whole horizon and deciding the issues of life on earth by their combined influences. The wind is as the "breath" of this earthly world in which we live, so that it represents the "breathing" of the cosmos. The breath is in a certain sense the vehicle of the "soul" or the "spirit," whence the etymological connection between these words in many languages; but it is also the active vehicle of life, for it nourishes and purifies the blood, life's passive, lower vehicle. The breath then, is thus both "soul" and "life" and thus it is made in the image of the Divine Word whose creative Breath made man himself.

*

*   *

As we have already mentioned, the cardinal points are associated symbolically with four Divinities which are referred to in many different ways, and which personify four complementary aspects of the universal Spirit; the Spirit unites these aspects in Itself as colors are unified in light; and this fourfold Spirit "is" *Wakan-Tanka* in the sense that it enjoys identity with God in virtue of the Oneness of Essence, just as light enjoys essential identity with the sun. According to the cosmology of the Sioux, each of these Divinities (or rather Semi-Divinities) is subdivided in its turn into four entities which rank one above the other in hierarchy and which are called by the most diverse names, such as Sun, Moon, Bison, Soul, each entity being an offshoot or reflection of the Spirit in the cosmos; these ramifications are in fact the secondary Angels whose numberless modalities penetrate as far as the confines of creation. The four Divine Powers may also clearly be conceived of as beyond manifestation, in the purely Principial Reality of *Wakan-Tanka*; they will then represent His fourfold Polarization, His Unity or Transcendence being always represented in the rite of the Calumet by the Sky; or in other words, the highest Angels are the reflections, in creation, of the essential Divine Qualities, so that the names of these Angels may be applied to these uncreated Qualities, and conversely.

In general, by reason of his polysynthetic or "vertical" perspective (we might say his "primordial" perspective) the Indian will tend to take a simultaneous view of the different hierarchized aspects of one and the same reality: he will tend to look on them as unified by their co-essentiality, so that, for example, the Earth will not be for him simply perceptible matter or simply the universal Substance, but both at the same time, the one in the other; the matter that his senses perceive will be for him the material appearance of the Divine Substance, thus the Divine Substance in its manifestation of materiality. This point of view shows itself in the very symbolism of the Thunderbird who is *Wakan-Tanka* as seen under the particular aspect of Revelation: like the thunderbolt, with which it is symbolically associated, the eagle pierces space, from Sky (of which it is the incarnation) to Earth; in other words, the Thunderbird forms a link, by its presence, between Heaven and all the lower degrees of "cosmic space."

But let us revert to the symbolism of the Four Winds: the Sioux draw an analogy between these and the four periods of the cycle, which are symbolized by the four eagle feathers that adorn the sacred hoop used in the Sun Dance and on other occasions: the first period is that of the Stone, the second that of the Bow, the third that of the Fire, and the fourth that of the Pipe, each of these symbols representing the spiritual means *(upāya)* characteristic of the respective period. There are likewise four ages through which every created thing must pass: the first is the South which is yellow and represents the source of all life, and this is the first age in a historical cycle; the second is the West, which is black; the third the North, which is white; and the fourth the East, which is red; earthly humanity is now in the fourth age which will end with a great disaster. This scheme of things which attributes the "Golden Age" to the South and the "Dark or Iron Age" to the East (whereas the other traditional doctrines attribute the "Golden Age" to the North and the "Iron Age" to the West) may seem at first surprising, but two things must here be taken into consideration: firstly, as regards the Golden Age (the *Krita-Yuga*), if it be correct to attribute it to the North — the earthly Paradise being, according to tradition, situated in the polar region — it is nonetheless true that in actual fact the North Pole is now covered with ice, and that in a qualitative sense the South[11] does really correspond to Paradise and thus to the Golden Age, so that the symbolism in question may be based on the warmth and fertility of the South just as well as on the Hyperborean situation of the Primordial Garden; secondly, as regards the Iron Age (the *Kali-Yuga*), if it be obviously correct to attribute it, according to the geographical perspective of the Old World, to the West, since it is there that the sun sets and there also that has arisen that final subversion which is spreading its shadows over the whole of humanity, it is nonetheless true that for the Indians this same subversion comes from the East; it is there that they situate what for the Orientals is the "dark West," and thence have come those "palefaced spirits" by whom the red race has been practically exterminated; but this does not prevent them from expecting that the universal Savior, the Messiah awaited by all peoples at the end of the Iron Age, will also come from the East, so that the solar symbolism of this direction remains intact in the Sioux theory of the four cyclic periods. Moreover, according to the cosmology of the Cheyenne Indians, the Primordial Tradition originally was established in the Arctic: the earthly Paradise lay in the far North on an island risen from the primordial waters; there, Spring was perpetual and men and animals spoke the same language. Then came tribulations (for example, two floods) after which the red race, or rather its primordial ancestors, settled definitively in the South which in its turn had become a fertile region.

11. This applies to the Northern hemisphere.

We must not forget to mention here that the Calumet has, besides its fourfold symbolism, a threefold one which relates to the three worlds and to which correspond respectively the sky, the cardinal points and the earth. The three worlds are also represented, among the Crow Indians, in the form of three rings painted on the central pole of the Sun Dance, this pole signifying the Tree of Life or the World Axis, in accordance with the Hyperborean symbolism;[12] they are then interpreted as making up the triad (in ascending order) body, soul, Spirit or gross, subtle, Pure.

*

* *

We now come to another aspect of the rite of the Calumet, and here may be seen the analogy between the smoke of the sacred tobacco *(kinnikinnik)* and incense: in most religions incense is as it were a human response to the Divine Presence[13] and the smoke marks the spiritual presence of man in the encounter with the supernatural[14] Pres-

12. "It should be remembered . . . that in diverse traditions the image of the Sun is also connected with the image of the tree, . . . being represented as the fruit of the 'World Tree'; it leaves its tree at the beginning of the cycle and comes back to rest there at the end so that : . . the tree is in fact 'the Station of the Sun.' " (René Guénon, "L'Arbre du Monde," in *Etudes Traditionnelles*, February, 1939.)

13. This Presence is symbolized among the Indians by the eagle feather; the eagle represents the Great Spirit.

14. This adjective is not a pleonasm, for the "natural" Presence of God is none other than Existence and its diverse expressions and forms, such as the symbols of Nature — Sun, Moon, Bison and others — which for the Indian are all *wakan*, sacred. — We will quote here the following deeply symbolic explanation which was given by an Indian chief to the well known ethnologist Alice C. Fletcher: "Everything as it moves, now and then, here and there, makes stops. The bird as it flies stops in one place to make its nest, and in another to rest in its flight. A man when he goes forth stops when he wills. So God has stopped. The sun, which is so bright and beautiful, is one place where He has stopped. The moon, the stars, the winds He has been with. The trees, the animals, are all where

ence of God, as is affirmed by this Iroquois incantation: "Hail! Hail! Hail! Thou Who has created all things, hear our voice. We are obeying Thy Commandments. That which Thou hast created returneth back unto Thee. The smoke of the holy plant riseth up unto Thee, whereby it may be seen that our speech is true."[15]

In the rite of the Calumet man represents the state of individuation; space (with its six directions) represents the Universal into which what is individual has — after being transmuted — to be reabsorbed; the smoke disappearing into space, with which it finally identifies itself, exemplifies well this transmutation from the hard, opaque or formal into the dissolved, transparent or formless; it exemplifies at the same time the unreality of the ego and so of the world which, spiritually, is identical with the human microcosm. But this resorption of the smoke into space (which stands for God) transcribes at the same time the Mystery of "Identity" in virtue of which, to use a Sufic expression, "the Sage is not created"; it is only in illusion that man is a volume cut out of space and isolated in it: in reality he "is" that space and he must "become what he is," as the Hindu Scriptures say.[16] By absorbing, together with the sacred

He has stopped, and the Indian thinks of these places and sends his prayers there to reach the place where God has stopped and win help and a blessing."

15. Quoted by Paul Radin in his *Histoire de la Civilisation Indienne*, Paris, Payot, 1953.

16. The symbolism of the Tibetan Buddhist "prayer wheel" is inversely analogous to that of the Calumet: whereas in relation to the Calumet, the Divine Reality is to be found in the directions of space towards which tend (starting from the center, which is the state of individuation) the spiritual aspirations of the individual, the "prayer wheel" represents the Divine Reality in the form of a revealed Utterance or *mantra* which is fixed in space by the sacred letters that transcribe it and which through its rotation blesses the Universe as manifested in space. According to an Upanishad: "*Brahma* is to the north, to the south, to the east, to the west, at the zenith and at the nadir." — In the same way the Koran says: "Wheresoever ye turn, there is the face of *Allāh*."

smoke, the perfume of Grace, and by breathing himself out with it towards the unlimited, man spreads himself supernaturally throughout the Divine Space, so to speak: but at the same time God is represented by the fire which consumes the tobacco. The tobacco itself represents man or, from the macrocosmic point of view, the Universe; space is here incarnate in the fire of the Calumet, just as, according to another symbolism, the cardinal points are united in the Central Fire.

*
*   *

According to Black Elk, "Everything an Indian does is done in a circle, and that is because the Power of the World always works in circles and everything tries to be round. In the old days when we were a strong and happy people, all our power came to us from the sacred hoop of the nation, and so long as the hoop was unbroken, the people flourished. The flowering tree was the living center of the hoop, and the circle of the four quarters nourished it. The East gave peace and light, the South gave warmth, the West gave rain, and the North with its cold and mighty wind gave strength and endurance. This knowledge came to us from the outer [transcendent or universal] World together with our religion. Everything the Power of the World does is done in a circle. The sky is round, and I have heard that the earth is round like a ball, and so are all the stars. The wind, in its greatest power, whirls. Birds make their nests in circles, for theirs is the same religion as ours . . . Our tipis were round like the nests of birds, and these were always set in a circle, the nation's hoop, a nest of many nests, where the Great Spirit meant us to hatch our children."[17]

All the static forms of existence, whether they be material or mental, are thus as it were determined by a concentric archetype: centered in his qualitative, "totemic," almost

17. *Black Elk Speaks*, op. cit.

impersonal ego, the Indian tends towards independence and so towards indifference with regard to the outward world; he surrounds himself with silence as with a magic circle, and this silence is sacred as being the vehicle of the heavenly influences. It is from this silence — of which the natural support is solitude — that the Indian draws his spiritual strength; his ordinary prayer is unvoiced: what it requires is not thought but consciousness of the Spirit, and this consciousness is immediate and formless like the vault of heaven.[18]

If the Great Spirit works always "in circles," He works also, in another respect, always "in fours," as may be seen from the directions of space and the cycles of time (and then the circle turns into the swastika, which is an important Red Indian symbol): that is why the Indian, whose course of life lies as it were between the central point and limitless space, makes static things according to the circular or unitive principle, and dynamic things (actions) according to the quaternary principle,[19] that is, in conformity with the four cardinal virtues which are for him: courage, patience, generosity and fidelity. This profound structure of Indian life signifies that the red man has no intention of fixing himself on this earth where everything, according to the law of stabilization and also of condensation (petrification, one might say) is liable to crystallize; and this explains the Indian's aversion for houses, especially stone ones, and

18. Needless to say, such an attitude of worship presupposes a mental heredity which no mere individual initiative could possibly replace.

19. The circle has also a dynamic symbolism, in relation to the cross considered in its static symbolism (we are not referring to the square — the static form par excellence — since it does not enter into this nomadic perspective). If the cross represents, not a centrifugal tendency, but the cardinal points, the circle will represent, not a concentric tendency, but the circular movement of the Four Winds about the world, that is, the passage of the four cosmic Principles from potency to act; the same image is to be found in the swastika, where the plain cross is obviously static and the hooks dynamic and rotatory.

also the absence of a writing which, from this perspective, would fix and kill the sacred flow of the Spirit. The European civilization, on the other hand, in both its dynamic and static forms, is thoroughly sedentary and urban: it is thus anchored in space where it spreads itself quantitatively, whereas the Indian civilization has its pivot as it were outside space in the unlocalized, principial center; its expansivity is therefore qualitative, in the sense that it is pure movement, symbolizing the limitless, and not a quantitative, not to say mercantile, setting of boundaries to the extension of space. It should be clearly understood in this connection that Christianity, like other religions of the Old World, establishes the Celestial on the earthly plane and builds sanctuaries in the most static of materials, stone; the religion of the Indians, on the other hand, integrates the earthly (the spatial) with the omnipresent Celestial, and that is why the red man's sanctuary is everywhere; that is also why the earth should remain intact, virgin and sacred, as when it left the Divine Hands — since only what is pure reflects the Eternal.[20] The Indian is nothing of a "panthe-

20. This perspective explains the great "nomadic revolutions" which, starting from the Mongolian steppes with an unheard of impetuosity, set out to sweep the towns — places of corruption and "petrification" — from the surface of the earth; there is much evidence to show that these conquerors were conscious of carrying out a Divine Decree. In any case, it cannot be denied that the materialistic and quantitative civilization of the modern world represents a peak of urban "incrustation," and that, but for sedentarism, such a civilization could never have come into existence; in fact it crushes nomadism everywhere, or rather, it crushes everything; it will end by crushing even itself. Let us add that the ring of Ghengiz Khan had on it the swastika which, as we have already mentioned, is also often to be found in the symbolic art of the Red Indians. As to the attitude of the Red Indian towards Nature on the one hand and cities on the other, Tacitus describes exactly analogous traits among the ancient Germans: "They think it would be degrading to the majesty of the Gods to imprison them between walls and to represent them by means of a human figure: they consecrate the woods and forests to them, and invoke, by the names of the divinities, that Mystery which they view solely

ist," nor does he imagine for one moment that God is in the world; but he knows that the world is mysteriously plunged in God.

What has just been said enables one to understand why Indian art is of an altogether primordial simplicity; its language is concentrated, direct and bold; like the Indian himself (a very noble human type and also one of the most powerfully original), his art is both qualitative and spontaneous; it is precise in its symbolism, while keeping at the same time a surprising freshness. It serves as a "framework" for man, and this explains the high quality of the Indian art of clothing: his majestic headdresses (above all, his great array of eagle feathers), his garments streaming with fringes and embroidered with solar symbols, the bright-patterned moccasins which seem designed to take away from the feet all heaviness and all uniformity, the feminine robes of an exquisite simplicity — this Red Indian art is certainly one of the most vigorous expressions of human genius.

We have seen that Nature (landscape, sky, stars, elements, wild animals) is a necessary support for the Indian tradition, just as temples are for other religions;[21] all the limitations imposed upon Nature by artificial, ponderous, immovable constructs (limitations that are likewise imposed upon man through his becoming a slave to these constructs) are thus sacrilegious, even "idolatrous," and

---

with reverential fear" (. . . *deorumque nominibus appellant Secretum illud, quod sola reverentia vident*). "It is well known that the Germans have no cities and will not even tolerate that their dwellings be touching one another." — Ammonius Marcellus, a fourth century author, reports that the Germans regarded the Roman cities with horror, as being prisons and tombs, and that, after having captured them, they abandoned them.

21. As a "Keeper of the Pipe" once said to Joseph Epes Brown, God shows His goodness by leaving Nature intact: "Although we have been crushed by the white man in every possible way, we still have much cause to be thankful to the Great Spirit, for even in this period of darkness His work in Nature remains unchanged and is a continual reminder of the Divine Presence."

they carry within themselves the seeds of death. Considered from this point of view the destiny of the red man is tragic in the true sense of the word — a tragedy being a desperate situation caused not by chance but by the fatal clash of two principles. The crushing of the Indian race is tragic because in its deepest and most intimate nature this noble people was opposed to "assimilation"; the red man could only conquer or die; it is the spiritual basis of this alternative which confers on the destiny of the red race an aspect of grandeur and martyrdom.[22] It was not simply because they were the weaker side that the Indians succumbed; they did so because they represented a nobility and a spirituality that was incompatible with the white man's commercialism[23] —

22. It is hard to say which was the more ignoble, the treacherous methods employed during the white expansion westwards, or the treatment inflicted on the Indians after their defeat. "The attempts to suppress native leadership and Indian social controls began under the agent who came to Pine Ridge in 1879 . . . Only through the acceptance of stock raising and settlement on farm tracts, he sincerely felt, could the Indian adjust to his new situation. However, like all people of his time, the agent also felt that this must be accompanied by a complete abandonment of Indian custom. Thus, when the Indians seemed to cling too tenaciously to camping by band groups, holding council by themselves, or being uncooperative, he withheld rations or utilized the police to force a change. . . . The undermining of native controls and native leadership was followed later by official regulations which forbade native dances, ceremonies, and pagan customs . . . Children were virtually kidnapped to force them into government schools, their hair was cut, and their Indian clothes thrown away. They were forbidden to speak in their own language . . . those who persisted in clinging to their old ways and those who ran away and were recaptured were thrown into jail. Parents who objected were also jailed. Where possible, children were kept in school year after year to avoid the influence of their families." (Gordon Macgregor, *Warriors without Weapons*, Chicago, University of Chicago Press, 1975.)

23. "Cain, who killed his brother, Abel, the herdsman, and built himself a city, prefigures modern civilization, one that has been described from within as a 'murderous machine, with no conscience and no ideals' (G. La Piana), 'neither human nor normal nor Christian' (Eric Gill), and in fact 'an anomaly, not to say a monstrosity' (René Guénon). It has been

because they embodied a character, an idea, a principle, and, being what they were, they could not be unfaithful to themselves. This great drama might be defined as the struggle, not only between a materialistic civilization and another that was chivalrous and spiritual, but also between urban civilization (in the strictly human and pejorative sense of this term, with all its implications of artifice and servility) and the kingdom of Nature considered as the majestic, pure, limitless raiment of the Divine Spirit. And it is from this idea of the final victory of Nature (final because it is primordial) that the Indians draw their inexhaustible patience in the face of the misfortunes of their race; Nature, of which they feel themselves to be embodiments, and which is at the same time their sanctuary, will end by conquering this artificial and sacrilegious world, for it is the Garment, the Breath, the very Hand of the Great Spirit.

said: 'The values of life are slowly ebbing. There remains the show of civilization, without any of its realities' (A. N. Whitehead). Criticisms such as these could be cited without end. Modern civilization, by its divorce from any principle, can be likened to a headless corpse of which the last motions are convulsive and insignificant. It is not, however, of suicide, but of murder that we propose to speak." (Ananda K. Coomaraswamy, *Am I My Brother's Keeper?*, Freeport, New York, Books for Libraries Press, 1967.) — "Savages we call them, because their manners differ from ours, which we think the perfection of civility; they think the same of theirs. . . . Having few artificial wants, they have abundance of leisure for improvement by conversation. Our laborious manner of life, compared with theirs, they esteem slavish and base; and the learning, on which we value ourselves, they regard as frivolous and useless." (Benjamin Franklin, *Remarks concerning the Savages of North America*, Dublin, printed for L. White, 1784.)

Gnosis, Language of the Self

There are various ways of expressing or defining the difference between gnosis and love — or between *jnāna* and *bhakti* — but here we wish to consider one criterion only, and it is this: for the volitional or affective man (the *bhakta*) God is "He" and the ego is "I," whereas for the gnostic or intellective man (the *jnānī*)[1] God is "I" — or "Self" — and the ego is "he" or "other."[2] It will also be immediately apparent why it is the former and not the latter perspective that determines all religious dogmatism: it is because the majority of men start out from certainty about the ego

1. We would readily say "the theosopher," if this word did not give rise to confusions. That the terms "gnostic" and "theosopher" have fallen into discredit is a bad sign, not, certainly, for men like Clement of Alexandria or Boehme who used them, but for the world which has occasioned and sanctioned such discredit. The same applies to the word "intellectual" the meaning of which has become something quite trivial. As for the term "pneumatic," it seems to us that it refers to realization alone, not to theory.

2. It is true that most of the sapiential doctrines, in taking account of the ego as a fact and inasmuch as they conform to "the letter" of the Revelation from which they derive, refer to the Absolute as "He" just like the dualists of the way of love, but this is hardly more than a question of dialectic which in no way modifies the fundamental perspective, as we have explained elsewhere: (See the chapter "*The Vedānta*"). Moreover the *Advaita Vedānta*, which is the most direct possible expression of gnosis, does not exclude "objectivist" formulations of the Principle, such as *Brahma, Shiva* and other divine Names.

rather than about the Absolute. Most men are individualists and consequently but little suited to concretely making an abstraction of their empirical "I," a process which is an intellectual problem and not a moral one: in other words, few have the gift of impersonal contemplation — for it is of this we are speaking — such as allows God to think in us, if such an expression be permissible.

The nature of pure intellection will be better understood from considering the following: the Intellect, which is One, presents itself in three fundamental aspects — at least insofar as we are situated in the "separative illusion" as is the case for every creature as such — namely, first the divine Intellect, which is Light and pure Act; secondly the cosmic intellect, which is a receptacle or mirror in relation to God and light in relation to man; and thirdly the human intellect, which is a mirror in relation to both of the foregoing and light in relation to the individual soul;[3] one must be careful, therefore, to distinguish in the intellect — the divine Intellect excepted — an uncreate aspect which is essential and a created aspect which is accidental or, rather, contingent.[4] This synthetic view of things results, one might say, from the principle of non-alterity: that which is not "other" in any respect is "identical" under the relationship being considered, so that intelligence as such — whether it be the intelligence of a man conforming to truth or that of a plant turning irresistibly towards light — "is" the intelligence of God; intelligence is "human" or "vegetable" only in relation to specific limitations, and similar considerations moreover apply to every positive quality, and there-

---

3. Sayings of the Gospel such as "I am the light of the world" or "No man cometh to the Father but by me" are applicable in all these three senses.

4. The mystery of the "universal Spirit" (*Ar-Rūh*) consists, in Islam, in not being able to say of it either that it is "created" or that it is "uncreate"; the same mystery is to be met with in the Intellect we have called "human" and which Meister Eckhart also defined in an ambiguous manner.

fore to all the virtues, which are always those of God, not of course in their belittling accidentality, but in their content or essence.

*

* *

From these considerations it can be seen that the great Gospel virtues — charity, humility, poverty, childlikeness — have their final end in the "Self":[5] they represent so many negations of that ontological inflation which is the ego, negations that are not individualistic and hence contradictory[6], but intellective; that is, their point of departure is the very Self, in conformity with the innermost nature of things. In a similar way, if a sage cannot be satisfied, in a final sense, with any created bliss — "the (created) Paradise is a prison for the Sufi" — this is not due to any pretension or ingratitude on his part, far from it, but because the Intellect tends towards its own Source, or because the Self in us "wants to be delivered." If Christ "is God," that is because the Intellect — "come down from Heaven" — is the Self; and in that sense, all genuine religions are "Christian": each one postulates on the one hand the uncreate Intellect — or the Logos, uncreate Word of God, which amounts to the same thing considering the "radiation" of the Intellect — and on the other hand it

---

5. The same could be said of the commandments of the Hebrew Decalogue: in the final analysis each one of them denotes an aspect of the Self and each transgression reveals an aspect of the ego as such. The "chosen people" corresponds to the soul that is "naturally" idolatrous and rebellious but has been "supernaturally" redeemed by the Messiah, who is Grace or Intellect.

6. A complex of guilt and a "set" attitude of humility are the commonest expressions of this contradiction. An attitude is false to the extent that it runs counter to truth; true humility, the kind that is most efficacious, is an impersonal "non-pride" which remains independent of the alternative "humiliation-flattery" and avoids all unhealthy preoccupation with the "I." Fundamental virtues are centered in God, not in man.

postulates the earthly manifestation of that Word and the deliverance it procures; every complete tradition postulates, in the final analysis, extinction of the ego in view of the divine "I," an extinction for which the sacred Law provides an elementary framework, although the Law must remain "dualistic" in its common letter to meet the needs of the majority and consequently for reasons of social psychology. "Inwardly" every religion is the doctrine of the one Self and its earthly manifestation, as also the path leading to the abolition of the false self, or the path of the mysterious reintegration of our "personality" into the celestial Prototype; "outwardly" the religions are "mythologies" or, to be more exact, symbolisms designed for differing human receptacles and displaying, by their limitations, not a contradiction *in divinis* but on the contrary a mercy. A doctrine or a Path is exoteric to the degree that it is obliged to take account of individualism — which is the fruit not so much of passion itself as of the hold exerted by passion upon thought — and to veil the equation of Intellect and Self under a mythological and moral imagery, irrespective of whether a historical element is combined with that imagery or not: and a doctrine is esoteric to the degree that it communicates the very essence of our universal position, our situation between nothingness and Infinity. Esoterism is concerned with the nature of things and not merely with our human eschatology; it views the Universe not from the human standpoint but from the "standpoint" of God.[7] The exoteric mentality, with its one-sided logic and its somewhat passional rationality, scarcely conceives that there are questions to which the answer is both "yes" and "no"; it is always afraid of falling into

7. "It is for certain chosen men, who have been allowed to pass from faith to gnosis, that the sacred mysteries of wisdom have been preserved under the veil of parables" (Clement of Alexandria, *Stromata*, VI, 126). This means, not that the parables do not contain a sense which is designed for all Christians while having to be hidden provisionally from unbelievers, but that they are

204

dualism, pantheism, quietism, and so on. In metaphysics as in psychology it is sometimes necessary to resort to ambiguous answers; for example, to the question: the world, "is it" God? we reply: "no," if by the "world" is understood ontological manifestation as such, that is to say in its aspect of existential or demiurgic separateness; "yes," if by "world" is understood manifestation insofar as it is causally or substantially divine, since nothing can be situated outside God; in the first case, God is exclusive and transcendent Principle, and in the second, total Reality or universal and inclusive Substance. God alone "is"; the world is a limited divine aspect, for it cannot — on pain of absurdity — be a nothingness on its own level. To affirm on the one hand that the world has no divine quality, and on the other that it is real apart from God and that it never ceases so to be, amounts to admitting two Divinities, two Realities, two Absolutes.

That which is "incarnation" for Christianity is "revelation" or "descent" for the other two monotheistic religions. The truth that only the divine manifestation "is the Self," to the exclusion of all human counterfeits, becomes exoterically: only such and such a divine manifestation — to the exclusion of all others — is the Self. It could also be said, on the plane of the microcosm, that the Intellect alone and no other human faculty — neither reason nor imagination nor memory nor feeling nor the faculties of sensory perception — is the Self although, viewed as existential structures, everything reflects or "is" the Self in some way or another. This exclusive value given to "incarnation" obviously also has, besides its spiritual significance, a historically literal meaning, which applies when one considers

at the same time the vehicles of a meaning that is genuinely gnostic or metaphysical, and thereby incomprehensible to the majority of Christians themselves. Christ's command not to cast pearls before swine nor to give what is sacred to dogs cannot have a meaning that is merely limited in time or reduced to a question of what is outwardly opportune.

the particular human cosmos where the divine manifestation has taken place, that is to say, in the case of Christ, the world of the Roman Empire and, in a still larger sense, the world of those whom the particular grace of Christ has "chosen," regardless of their country of origin; but the literalistic interpretation becomes unacceptable as soon as an attempt is made to add some fact or other, be it even a sacred fact, to metaphysical truth, as if the latter were incomplete without it — whereas all possible facts are already included in that truth — and as if metaphysical truth were subject to time. To take another example: the Koranic affirmation that "God alone is God" means that there is no Self but the Self; exoterically however this statement implies that God could not manifest Himself as such "outside Himself," which amounts to rejecting the phenomenon of incarnation; but in every case of this kind, esoterism restores the total truth on the plane of principles. In short, the difference between Christian and Islamic gnosis is essentially this: whereas Christian gnosis projects the mystery of the God-man — and thereby the mystery of the Trinity — into the soul of the gnostic, as is shown for example by certain Eckhartian texts, Sufism, for its part, sees "unification" *(tawḥīd)* or the "unity of Existence" or rather the unity of Universal Reality *(waḥdat Al-Wujūd,* sometimes translated as "Supreme Identity") as resulting from the very nature of the Divine Unity.[8]

The exoteric distinction between "the true religion" and "false religions" is replaced, for the gnostic, by the distinction between gnosis and creeds, or between essence and

---

8. The Islamic formula *Lā ilāha illā 'Llāh* means, according to gnosis, that "there is no 'me' except it be 'I' " — therefore no real or positive ego except the Self — a meaning which also springs from expressions such as the *Anā 'l-Ḥaqq* ("I am the Truth") of Al Hallaj or the *Subḥānī* ("Glory to Me") of Bayezid. The Prophet himself enunciated the same mystery in the following terms: "He who has seen me, has seen the Truth (God)." (That is to say: God cannot be seen except through His receptacle or, in a more general but less direct sense, through His symbol), and also: "I am

forms.[9] The sapiential perspective alone is an esoterism in the absolute sense, or in other words, it alone is necessarily and integrally esoteric, because it alone transcends all relativities.

*

* *

God is "Light" "before" He is "Heat," if it may be so expressed; gnosis "precedes" love, or rather, love "follows" gnosis, since the latter includes love after its own fashion, whereas love is not other than the beatitude that has "come forth" from gnosis. One can love something false, without love ceasing to be what it is; but one cannot "know" the false in a similar way, that is to say knowledge cannot be under illusion as to its object without ceasing to be what it is; error always implies a privation of knowledge, whereas sin does not imply a privation of will. Therein lies a most important application of the symbolism of the Adamic androgyne and of the creation of Eve: it is only after the "coming forth" of love outside knowledge — whence the polarization of "intelligence" and "will" — that the temptation and fall could — or can — take place; in one sense, the rational faculty became detached from Intellect through the intrusion of will, seduced by "the serpent" and become "free" from below, that is to say rendered capable of making choice between true and false; choice of the false having once become possible, it was bound to present itself as a seduction of torrential force; reason, mother of the "wisdom according to the flesh" is the "natural child"

He and He is I, save that I am who I am, and He is who He is." — "I have been charged with fulfilling my mission since the best of the ages of Adam (the origins of the world), from one age to another until this age where I am."

9. If in relation to the pole "subject" gnosis is the doctrine of the Self, in relation to the pole "object" it will be the doctrine of the Essence: "That Knowledge which sees the One Indestructible in all beings, the One Indivisible in all separate lives, may be truly called Pure Knowledge." (*Bhagavad-Gītā*, XVIII, 20.)

issued from Adam's sin. Here the serpent represents what Hindus understand by *tamas*, that tendency which is "downward," "towards obscurity," "compressive" and at the same time "dispersive" and "dissolving" and which on contact with the human person becomes personified as Satan. The question: "why does evil exist?" amounts, in short, to asking why there is an existence; the serpent is to be found in Paradise because Paradise exists. Paradise without the serpent would be God.

*

*   *

Man complains of his sufferings, such as separation and death; but has he not inflicted them a priori upon the Self, by his very egoity? Is not individuation a separation from the divine "I" and is not the ego itself a death with regard to infinite Life? It will be objected that we are not responsible for our existence; but man ceaselessly recreates, in his actions, this responsibility which he thinks he does not bear; in this, taken together with the foregoing considerations, lies the deeper meaning of original sin.[10] Man suffers because he wishes to be "self" in opposition to "the Self," and Christ effaces this fundamental sin by taking on Him-

10. There are some apparent heresies that are not false in themselves, but which refer to an "ontological stratum" lying deeper than that of ordinary theological concepts: the refusal to attribute an absolute validity to "original sin" proceeds, when it has an adequate motive, from a more fundamental and more "neutral" vision of our human reality, one which however is less accessible to a given mentality and therefore also less opportune for a given morality; similarly, "quietism," insofar as it contains a legitimate element, stands nearer to contemplation and gnosis than does the accumulating of merits; "there is no lustral water like unto Knowledge," says the Law of Manu. It can be regretted, without departing from realism, that Western theology has not known a grading of truths according to differing levels of validity: having chosen but one level, more or less, namely the level of what was opportune for the collectivity, this theology firstly impoverished itself and then indirectly provoked "explosions" which have ended by threatening its very existence.

self the suffering resulting from it. He is the Self holding out a hand to "me"; man must lose his life, the life of the ego, in order to keep it, the life of the Self. Under His solar aspect — implying the warmth of love as also the light of wisdom — Christ is the Self that unites and absorbs all beings. The Self became ego in order that the ego might become the Self; the divine "Subject" became cosmic "object" because the "object" must once again become "subject."[11] The Self alone is "itself"; the ego is "other," hence its initial unbalance and its insatiability: it never ceases its search for itself; in whatever it does, it is in pursuit of that transcendent and absolute "Me" in which the beatitudes are inward and definitive instead of being scattered throughout an endlessly deceptive world. "The Kingdom of God is with you."

If "that which is born of the Spirit is spirit," this is because Spirit is the Self and because there is no other knowing or loving Subject in infinite Beatitude; similarly, if he who is "born of the Spirit"[12] is like the wind of which

11. "And the light shineth in darkness; and the darkness comprehended it not": the ego has not understood that its immortal reality — or that the Intellect — is none other than the Self. "That which ye shall have done to one of these little ones, have ye done unto Me": this is the enunciation, as Coomaraswamy so justly remarked, of the cosmic reverberation of the Self, who is "the one and only transmigrant" according to Shankara.

12. "Except a man be born of water and of the Spirit he cannot enter the kingdom of God. That which is born of the flesh is flesh; and that which is born of the Spirit is spirit" (John III, 3-7). — "Water is looked on by many traditions as the original medium of beings, and the reason lies in its symbolism . . . by which water represents *Mūla Prakriti*; in a superior sense and by transposition, water is Universal Possibility itself; he who is 'born of water' becomes a 'son of the Virgin,' therefore also an adopted brother of Christ and co-heir to the Kingdom of God. Besides, if one observes the fact that 'spirit'. . . is the Hebrew *Ruahh* (here associated with water as a complementary principle, as at the beginning of Genesis) and that *Ruahh* at the same time corresponds to air, one will recognize in this the idea of purification by the elements. . . ." (René Guénon, *Man and His Becoming According to the Vedanta*, Chapter XXI, footnote.)

"thou canst not tell whence it cometh, and whither it goeth," this is because, being identified with the Self, he is without origin; he has come forth from the chain of cosmic causations and dwells in the Changeless. Similarly again, a reference to the Self — apart from other meanings — is to be seen in these words: "None has gone up to Heaven but he who came down from Heaven. . . ." To "go up to Heaven" is to "become Oneself," that is to say, to become that which one has never really ceased to be, in the sense that the essence of the ego is the Self, that "Life" which we can procure only by losing the life of "me."[13]

For Socrates, in Plato's dialogues, the "true philosopher" is one who consecrates himself to "studying the separation of soul from body, or the liberation of the soul," and "who is always occupied in the practice of dying"; it is one who withdraws from the bodily — and therefore from all that, in the ego, is the shadow or echo of the surrounding world — in order to be nothing other than absolutely pure Soul, immortal Soul, Self: "The Soul-in-itself must contemplate Things-in-themselves" *(Phaedo)*. Thus the criterion of truth — and the basis of conviction, this reverberation of Light in the "outer man" — is Truth in itself, the prephenomenal Intelligence by which "all things were made" and without which "nothing was made that was made."

*

*　*

We have said previously that, in the human microcosm, only the Intellect "is" the Self, and not any specifically

---

13. "With Christ I must be buried," said St. Gregory of Nazianza, "with Christ I must rise again, and with Christ I must inherit; I must become Son of God and God himself" *(Sermon,* VII, 23). "Understand who has given you to be Son of God, heir of Christ, and — to use a bold term — God himself" (Ibid., XIV, 23). — "But this (the Kingdom of Heaven) consists, in my view, in nothing but the possession of what is most pure and most perfect. But the most perfect thing that exists is Knowledge of God" (Ibid., XX, 12).

mental faculty. For just as a distinction has to be made between an ordinary creature and "the Word made flesh," so also it is necessary to distinguish between rational thought, which is discursive and proceeds from the mental faculty alone, and intellective thought, which proceeds from intuition and pure Intellect: this second mode of thought is, in effect, an "exteriorization in view of an interiorization," whereas the first is purely and simply an expression in view of manifestation as such. To rational thought there corresponds the infra-human world, production of the "cosmic brain," and to intellective thought there corresponds the human species, expression of the "heart"; on a smaller scale and within the framework of humanity itself, it is the *Avatāra* who corresponds to this second mode of thought. The whole Christ-enacted drama, or the drama of Revelation itself, is thus prefigured — or else "post-figured," according to the point of view — in the intellectual act, either in the original intellection itself or in unitive meditation; this form of thought is like a "saving" or "unitive incarnation" of the Heart-Intellect. In other words, a distinction has to be made between terrestrial thought, given rise to by the environment and finding its end within the environment, and celestial thought given rise to by that which is our eternal substance and finding its end beyond ourselves and, in the final analysis, in the Self. Reason is something like a "profane intelligence"; essentially the profane point of view springs from it. It is necessary for reason to be determined, transfigured or regenerated, either by faith or by gnosis, which is the quintessence of faith.

Gnosis, by the very fact that it is a knowing and not a willing, is centered in "that which is" and not in "that which ought to be"; there results from this a way of regarding the world and life that is greatly different from the way, more "meritorious" perhaps but less "true," in which predominantly volitive minds regard the vicissitudes of existence. The background of the drama of life is, for the *bhakta,* the "Will of God" and, for the *jnānī,* the nature of things; the accepting of his fate results, for the former, from unconditional love, from "that which must be"; for the latter, acceptance results from discernment of metaphysical necessity, therefore, from "that which is." The *bhakta* accepts all fate as coming from the Beloved; he also accepts it because he makes no distinction between "me" and "others" and because, by this very fact, he cannot rebel against an event merely because it has happened to himself and not to some other person; if he accepts everything out of love of God, he also does so, on this same basis, out of love of his neighbor. The attitude of the *jnānī,* on the other hand, is an impassability founded upon discernment between the Real and the unreal: "The world is false, *Brahma* is true"; "That art thou" *(Tat Tvam Asi);* "All is *Ātmā* "; "I am *Brahma.*" Events of life arise, as do all phenomena, out of the indefinitely varying combinations of the three "cosmic qualities" (the *gunas: sattva, rajas* and *tamas);* these events therefore cannot but be, to the extent that the world is relatively real; but as soon as that relativity is transcended, they cease to exist and then there is no longer a "good" or an "evil," nor any karmic causation; the plane of the *gunas* ("simultaneous" qualities) and of *karma* (made up of "successive" qualities) is as if annihilated in the undifferentiated serenity of Being or of the Self. And similarly, there is no "juridical" relationship between the astonishments, anxieties and indignations of the soul and the unconditional serenity of the Intellect, or to be more precise, between the logic of anxiety and the transcendence of serenity; the gap is incommensurable and yet the second term is already hidden within the first; it is, so to speak, already within reach.

In spiritual life, he who says "to will" says "to will a Good"; "to will a Good" is "to will well," that is to say to "will through the Good," or "through God"; instead of "to will" one could also say "to love" and instead of "the Good" one could say "the Beautiful." On the other hand, he who says "to know" says "to know that which is"; he who says "to know that which is," says, in a final analysis, "to be that which knows": the Self.

*

* *

Reference has been made to the "cosmic qualities," the *gunas,* and to *karma,* as well as to the serenity which transcends all conditions of existence: this serenity — or this deliverance — lies in a certain way at the center of existence like a kernel of peace and light; it is like a drop of redemptive dew in an ocean of flames. "The whole universe is on fire," said the Buddha; our misfortune lies in our not knowing that the substance of existence is fire, this substance into which we are woven while yet remaining alien bodies. For the "naive" and "unrepentant" man, the world is a neutral space from which he chooses the agreeable contents while believing he can avoid the disagreeable, provided he be clever and meet with good luck; now the man who does not know that existence is an immense brazier has no imperative reason for wanting to get out of it, and that is why an Arab proverb says, "The beginning of wisdom is the fear of God" — that is to say, the fear of divine afflictions, which are the price of our state of remoteness.

The kernel of light at the center of the current of forms is essentially the "remembrance of God" — which in the end demands all that we are — as these sayings of Muhammad declare: "All that is to be found on earth is accursed, save only the remembrance of God," and: "There is no fault greater than existence." "None is good but one: God," said Christ: this implies that what comes from God — His Name — and what leads to Him — remembering Him — share in His goodness. The virtual fire from which we live withdraws from things to the very extent that we are centered on the mystery of this remembrance; things then become transparent and transmit to us the rays of their immutable and blessed archetypes. We could also say that

213

existence is fire insofar as it is regarded as being outside God and, by this fact, it also leads to fire; it is a burning for the perverted will and illumination for the contemplative intelligence, and it is thus at once threat and "consolation," enslaving seduction and liberating vision. It is the immutable and blessed archetypes that man is seeking when he attaches himself to shadows here below; and he suffers cruelly, first when these shadows disappear and later when, at death, he perceives the archetypes, from which his love for shadows had turned him away.[14]

In its all-comprehensive reality, Existence is serene and not maleficent; the cosmic Wrath is reabsorbed into total and virginal Equilibrium. Existence in itself is the universal Virgin who conquers, by her purity as also by her mercy, the sin of the demiurgic Eve, producer of creatures and of passions; Eve, who brings forth, seduces and attaches, is "eternally" conquered by the Virgin who purifies, forgives and liberates.

For gnosis, the existential fire is inseparable from ignorance and so from illusion. The fundamental cause of illusion or of ignorance is not however our state of fall nor some deficiency of the existential substance, but the principle of objectification, by which the pole "being" is cut off from the pure Subject; seen from this angle, the universal Virgin also is "illusory," and even Being is illusory insofar as it is distinct from the supra-ontological Subject which is the Self.[15] But Existence and Being, while still belonging to the realm of *Māyā*, nonetheless remain beyond the current of forms, and in consequence beyond separation, suffering and death.

14. Music — as well as dancing — is the art of bringing terrestrial shadows back to celestial vibrations and divine archetypes. In the plastic arts an analogous function is performed by stylization.

15. In Eckhart, Silesius, Omar Khayyam and others, allusions are found to this "relativity" of Being in relation to the Self. In the doctrines of India and the Far East — in *Advaita Vedānta*, Mahayana Buddhism and Taoism — this idea is fundamental.

Gnosis, it must be repeated, is our participation — however precarious and conditional, yet possible since we could not be in every respect absolutely "distinct" from God, since otherwise we would be devoid of reality — gnosis, then, is our participation in the "perspective" of the divine Subject which, in turn, dwells beyond the separative polarity "subject-object," which however in no way signifies that it does not bear within itself, in a manner conforming with its Essence, the cause of all cosmic polarizations; this means that we can indeed discern something like a polarity in it, but on condition of not seeing there any separation or opposition.

*

*   *

The Absolute Subject bears its immediate and connatural Object within itself and that Object is infinite Beatitude. When the Hindu doctrine describes *Ātmā* as being made of "Being," "Consciousness" and "Beatitude" (*Sat, Chit, Ānanda*, whence the divine Name *Sachchidānanda*) this enumeration means that the Subject is "Being that knows, having Beatitude for its object": being, or being real — It is "Consciousness" of all its own possibilities; the use of the verb "to be" here is quite provisional, since the Self is situated beyond ontological Unity. Now, the world is as it were included in the divine Beatitude, or more precisely, it is as if included in Being which is so to speak the outward dimension of Beatitude or the Self; we say "outward" inasmuch as we place ourselves at the standpoint of the world which is that of man, for it goes without saying that there is no "outwardness" in the Infinite. And, that is why it is said in theology that God has created the world "by goodness": "love" and "goodness" as also "beauty" are so many aspects of Beatitude, which is identified with All-Possibility. That the world is "contained" in the divine Beatitude or Goodness means, in relation to suffering — even in hell — that the creature always keeps the gift, positive in itself, of existence and that all suffering necessarily is limited in its nature and duration, God alone being absolute.

The subjective principle emanating from the divine Subject traverses the Universe like a ray, ending in the multitude of egos. The formal world is characterized by the outward limits of its contents, therefore by a kind of indefinite segmentation:[16] its "subjectivity" will thus be multiple, whence the innumerable diversity of souls. Man marks, for the terrestrial world that is his, the limit of the creative ray; man's sufficient reason is to be this limit, in other words, to stop, after the manner of an echo or a mirror, the "ray of exteriorization" of the Self; thus the human state is a gate of exit — and the only gate for the terrestrial world — not merely out of this world or of the formal cosmos, but even out of the immense and countless objectification that is universal Existence; being a total microcosm, a "plenary I,"[17] the human state is at the same time a door open towards the Self and immortality.

Is there any immortality outside the Self? Yes and no. There is also paradisiacal immortality, but the latter comes to an end — "upwards" — in the final reintegration (the *mahāpralaya* of the Hindus, or the end of a "day of *Brahma*") of Existence in the Self; but this ending, precisely, is a "more" and not a "less," a fulfilling *in divinis* and not an abolition.

*

* *

In one of his hymns to *Hari*, Shri Shankaracharya says: "Lord, although I and thou make but One, I belong to Thee, but not Thou to me, just as the waves belong to the

---

16. In the nonformal or supra-formal world, which is the realm of the angelic states, all things are perceived as subsisting "within" the subject, differences among the angelic subjects being marked by their modes of perception.

17. And not a partial "I" such as is, for instance, an animal ego.

sea, but not the sea to the waves." And in another hymn, Shankara expresses himself thus: "That which is the cessation of mental agitation and the supreme peace; that which is the lake *Manikarnika* and the pilgrimage of pilgrimages; that which is the primordial, most pure Ganges, the river of Knowledge; that is Benares, inborn Wisdom, and that is what I am."

INDEX

Index

Esoterism as Principle and as Way,
Perennial Books, 1981, 1990

Castes and Races,
Perennial Books, 1959, 1982

Sufism: Veil and Quintessence,
World Wisdom Books, 1981

From the Divine to the Human,
World Wisdom Books, 1982

Christianity/Islam,
World Wisdom Books, 1985
Select Books, 1996

The Essential Writings of Frithjof Schuon (S.H. Nasr, Ed.),
Amity House, 1986
Element, 1991

Survey of Metaphysics and Esoterism,
World Wisdom Books, 1986

In the Face of the Absolute,
World Wisdom Books, 1989, 1994

The Feathered Sun: Plain Indians in Art & Philosophy,
World Wisdom Books, 1990

To Have a Center,
World Wisdom Books, 1990

Roots of the Human Condition,
World Wisdom Books, 1991

Images of Primordial & Mystic Beauty: Paintings by Frithjof Schuon,
Abodes, 1992

Echoes of Perennial Wisdom,
World Wisdom Books, 1992

The Play of Masks,
World Wisdom Books, 1992

Road to the Heart,
World Wisdom Books, 1995

The Transfiguration of Man,
World Wisdom Books, 1995

The Eye of the Heart,
World Wisdom Books, 1997